D0583500

ANTHROPOLOGICAL
STRUCTURES
OF
MADNESS
IN BLACK AFRICA

ANTHROPOLOGICAL STRUCTURES OF MADNESS IN BLACK AFRICA

I. Sow

translated by
Joyce Diamanti

INTERNATIONAL UNIVERSITIES PRESS, INC.
New York

Library of Congress Cataloging in Publication Data

Sow, Alfâ Ibrâbîm.
    Anthropological structures of madness in Black Africa.
    Translation of Les structures anthropologiques de la folie en Afrique Noire.
    Bibliography: p.
    1. Psychiatry, Transcultural — Africa, Sub-Saharan.
2. Psychology, Pathological — Classification — Africa, Sub-Saharan. 3. Psychotherapy — Africa, Sub-Saharan.
4. Personality and culture — Africa, Sub-Saharan.
I. Title.
RC451.A438S6813   362.2'0422'0967   80-13909
ISBN 0-8236-0385-7

To my parents,
with respect
and infinite gratitude

Contents

Introduction

The present study, as its title indicates, is intended as the anthropological complement of my book on dynamic psychiatry in Black Africa (I. Sow, 1977). In that earlier work I reached the conclusion that a coherent psychopathology — a theoretical foundation necessary to any system of psychiatry really worthy of the name — must draw the substance of its theory from the same vital sources that form the elements of the personality. What I am trying to say is that there can be no valid psychiatric theory or, *a fortiori*, doctrine that is not based on the the institutional framework and symbolic spaces that effectively bring about the integration of elements of the personality, but that also shed light on the processes of disintegration of the personality.

Classical Western nosography, therefore, if it is

conceived of as a fixed set of immutable, nominalist categories, seems inadequate to provide a coherent description of the complex clinical realities observed in research fieldwork. Let me make one point clear: What I am throwing into question here is not classification per se, as a principle — indeed, all understanding begins from there. Nevertheless it seems clear, even with Western patients, that classical nosography has become outdated; in practicing his profession, every clinician discovers its obsolescence and its limitations. Fundamentally related to this phenomenon is the fact that classical Western nosology itself — on which nosographic descriptions and categories are based — is in a state of upheaval. In effect, under the influence of the evolution of Western societies themselves, combined with the impact of internal theoretical movements (such as psychoanalysis, phenomenology, etc.), a veritable crisis has arisen in Western psychiatry, and, in particular, a profound questioning of the very concept of mental illness.

The truth of the matter is that classical nosology — and consequently classical nosography — derived its validity from seemingly fixed clinical data, which refer to psychological, cultural, social, and familial realities of what is now another era. In the West today, sociocultural guidelines seem to be less well defined and established frames of reference less stable than they were at the end of the nineteenth century and the beginning of the twentieth. In other words, all our everyday experience suggests that in our professional practice we continue to use the classical nosographic categories superficially — sometimes mechanically — in order to "fix" into patterns what is in ceaseless dynamic flux. In this second half of the twentieth century, clinical cases seem to the practitioner to be infinitely more "mobile" and more complex, and the descriptive categories, deriving from a period of apparent psychocultural constancy, prove incapable of capturing the current clinical picture. More fundamentally, at the nosological level, I contend that the present period of disintegration of "classical" cultural ties, if only we look carefully enough, can teach us more about Western man — about his existential anxieties and his profound uncertainties, about the origins and growth of mental illness in his relation to the real parameters of his life — than do periods of apparent stability in which everything seems fixed in a trouble-free eternity.

Although that argument forms the major thrust of the present study, I propose first to make a critical analysis of classical Western nosography in its systematic application to African patients suffering from mental disorders. Then, by examining the status and functions of the traditional practitioner as a uniquely privileged "informant," I shall try to show the interrelationships that exist between such factors as psychiatric nosography/nosology, the concept of person/personality, and the place of the psychiatrist and what is expected of him in any sociocultural system.

The African conception of madness is a molar conception (rather than an analytical and/or molecular one) that falls within a broader dynamic anthropological perspective. As I described in detail in *Psychiatrie dynamique africaine* (I. Sow, 1977), it is based on the fundamental notion of conflict in the underlying relational networks that give structure to the whole of a person's daily life. Thus the traditional African practitioner — the same as a Western psychoanalyst, in a way — is first of all a diagnostician regarding the coherence of the structure that constitutes the personality. Next, one like the other, both are specialists in the field of relational conflict (interpretation, then resolution). Lastly, in terms of general method of investigation, both take as their point of departure the content of certain clinical phenomena — dreams, hallucinations (or fantasies), etc., so many symptoms to be deciphered — and proceed from signifier to signifier until reaching the end of the symbolic chain of signifiers. At this point it becomes possible to formulate the problem semantically, for madness is always a real-life drama, the strands of which must be unraveled in order to reestablish mental coherence. That is why, at the technical level, the education of the traditional practitioner — with its dramatically experienced stages of initiation, during training and under posttraining supervision — can be broadly compared to that of the Western psychoanalyst.

Nevertheless, in more concrete terms, the status and functions of the traditional therapist become intelligible only when related to the anthropological framework that shapes the particular idea of personality in which he is a specialist. Indeed, we should always bear in mind that the competent traditional therapist — just like the Western psychoanalyst in Western culture — is someone "in the know," an initiate who is knowledgeable about the most fundamental elements and symbols of the person/personality. As such, both are thought to have achieved that state (by paying with their own personal essence) and to be able to make their patients achieve it. Therefore, through (and in) their practice, not only do they interpret the culture but, much more, they help to reinforce it in individuals. Indeed, any form of psychotherapy that is well conceived and well conducted — no matter what else might be said of it — consists in strengthening the coherence of the patient's personality, always in terms of a model that is neither as neutral nor as "individual" as some would have us believe.

For this reason, in the third chapter of the present study I have tried to trace the sociocultural parameters of experience of the self in traditional society, parameters that form general frames of reference, constituting a guide for the education of children and adolescents as well as containing principles for the codification of adult behavior. We can distinguish, in theory, three orders of hierarchical reality, although in practice they are intertwined in daily life. What could be called the *macrocosmos* links transcendence and immanence: in another vocabulary, it is the rational and enveloping universe of Being, of Order, and of the Signified (Ancestor, Law, the founding Act, the initiatory Word), before which there was, "once upon a time," only chaos (absence of meaning, blind chance), because indifferentiation reigned, breeding diffuse violence. In terms of individuality and community, there was, at that time, neither classification nor any precise identity for each thing, each being — in short, it was an impenetrable, teeming, wordless world, without order or law save that of the "natural" violence of chance.

Today, and since the dawning of culture, this chaotic world has been pushed into the background, a hidden, intermediate order, which I have named the *mesocosmos*. In terms of traditional African themes, the mesocosmos is a place devoid of culture, the domain of doubles who are the "natural" twins of human beings. And mesocosmic society is a doubles' society, for it functions as an invisible replica, or duplicate, of the visible society of real men. In practical terms, the mesocosmos has become the place that gives rise to all good and bad fortune, the site of dramatic events as well as the source of worldly success. That is why it can be called the "structured collective imaginary," for it is the space that gives form to the desires, fears, anxieties, and hopes for success in the ups and downs of daily life; it is both reservoir and crucible of the collective imaginary for present and future cultural creations. According to traditional themes, the day-to-day psychological fate of individual human beings is modulated by a subtle dialectic of complex (often ambiguous) relations between humans and the creatures of this mesocosmos (African genies or spirits): invisible but powerful, good or bad, gratifying or persecutory — and, as such, they can drive one mad. Similarly traceable to this collective imaginary is the efficacy of antisocial affects (hate, jealousy, rancor, etc.) when they become destructive of the personality.

In the fourth chapter of this study, I have attempted to analyze certain mythic African themes, without which, as a matter of fact, nothing fundamental could be said about Africans (or consequently about madness in Africa). Further long and detailed studies will be required, of course, before we succeed in tying into a coherent whole the long chain leading from primordial symbols and words to everyday behaviors and vice versa. Mental illness, in all its diverse manifestations, will become truly comprehensible only when we manage to situate it in relation to this long chain of signifiers.

Lastly, the *microcosmos* (the third order of reality of the panstructured African universe) can be described as the immediate and apparent world of everyday social life. It is organized, needless to say, in complete conformity with the macrocosmos; indeed, the true words or principles of society, which dictate all sociocultural praxis, have their source in the fundamental law of the Ancestor. At the same time, however, the microcosmos works in full complicity and complexity with the mesocosmos, following the practice of playing it safe in the matter of relations. Be that as it may, the relational complex that is established, based on the order of the founding Ancestor, defines in a precise way the frames of reference of each person's identity within lineages, groups, and subgroups, as well as all the possible configurations — not indeterminate in number — of meaningful sociocultural relationships. Within this vast ensemble, prohibitions are delineated and specified that serve to bar a return to the original chaos, to indiscriminate violence, which destroys the cultural bond and hence personal identity, generating madness and constant insecurity for all. In the final analysis, it could well be that anomie, in its African context, simply expresses a deep-seated vacillation with respect to fixing the underlying reference points of identification, or, in other words, too great a gap between the collective value systems related to the idea of personhood (systems that are becoming extinct) and the narcissistic (and fortuitous) expressions of the individual personality that has no other model or end than itself.

One of the lessons that the psychiatrist can learn from live investigation in the field and from modern anthropological research is that he must belong to his time and place, serving the people of his time and place. For that, he must keep in constant touch with the indigenous sources that give structure to — but also with the conditions that bring destruction to — the subtle and complex ordering of the psychic life of those who are now his patients. Earlier, he will have critically weighed the fundamental principles (and validity) of his calling, at the same time equipping himself with conceptual tools that are consonant with actual historical developments. This revised conceptual battery can be envisaged only in terms of a nosology that is perceived to be dynamic, in contrast to a nosology of fixed entities, cut and dried, purely idiopathic and nominalist in nature, as nosology is still all too likely to be taught to students today.

CHAPTER ONE

Theoretical Problems Raised by the Use of Western Nosology in African Psychiatry

In this chapter I shall examine the problem of applying Western nosological categories to the study of
mental disorders in Black Africa, outlining its
theoretical and methodological implications. Beyond
all the ramifications of the discussion that follows, what
I hope to bring out are the underlying lines of correspondence, in a particular socioculture, between the
nosological picture, the nosographic organization of
psychopathological phenomena, and the overall an-

thropological perspective, which in turn encompasses
the conception of both an individual and an illness.

To date, in practice as well as in research, the
methodological order has been to start out with Western
nosological constructions and then, with the help of
nosographic pictures and patterns, to collect field data
in the form of symptoms and organize them into syndrome constellations and disorders that conform to the
pictures and patterns derived from Western experience
with mental illness. In the domain of African research
and practice, however, it is my hope to contribute to the
construction of a psychiatric nosology that is formulated
in the light of African anthropological structures.

To facilitate understanding of this change of orientation as compared to the classical approach, in the discussion that follows I have used the studies of Western
psychiatrists to present the various manifestations of
mental morbidity — precisely in terms of Western
nosography — in one particular sector: the Western-
type hospital. Thus we shall be considering a specific
category of patients, to the extent that they meet, more
or less, the usual criteria for psychiatric hospitalization
in the West.[1]

To demonstrate the difficulties encountered in coming
to grips with the subject, I am going to ask the reader to
join me in a rapid survey in which — by applying to these
hospital patients (inpatients or outpatients) precisely the
broad nosographic categories derived from classical

[1]For further details concerning the various modes of admission to
modern hospitals, as well as the causes and implications of hospitalization,
the reader is referred to the informative study of Storper-Perez (1968) on
hospitalization among the Wolof of Senegal.

Western nosology — we shall identify the principal practical, theoretical, and clinical problems that present themselves daily to psychiatrists in Western-type therapeutic centers.

In reviewing the comprehensive studies that have been conducted using Western psychiatric guidelines, I should like to point out and stress from the start that the complexity of the task is aggravated not only by the different terminologies used but also by the conceptual disparities that exist in Western psychiatric thinking itself. Also, the studies carried out in various regions of Africa in different Western languages reflect, at the same time, their contradictions and divergent nosological orientations — in particular, with respect to the important and difficult question of schizophrenia.[2]

What I have purposely tried to do here is to present an overall panorama rather than a comparative study in the strict sense, which would not fall within our area of concern. I therefore begin with the most common concepts of Western psychiatry to determine the psychiatric situation in Africa as it appears in the sector of hospitalization or Western-type treatment, and also as it emerges from the various field studies that have been carried out to date.

There is no doubt that in terms of the normal criteria, theoretically as well as practically, African patients who are hospitalized in the modern sector (i.e., outside the traditional milieu) are indeed sick in the sense of

[2]By "languages" I mean not only the various Western tongues, conveying differences of nosological classification, but also the transposition to Africa of the theoretical perspectives of the various schools, such as psychoanalysis, structuralism, evolutionist neoorganicism, etc.

Western psychiatry, and for a threefold reason.

First, a request to be taken into care has been made by the patient himself, by his family group, or by a responsible administrative authority.

Next, his clinical picture seems to correspond (more or less) to some international nosographic category: otherwise, he would not be sick in the view of the Western-type psychiatric center to which he has been admitted. Nevertheless, such hospitalization, despite the criteria applied on the nosographic as well as the nosological level, gives no indication of what mental illness might consist of in traditional surroundings. Moreover, as any psychiatrist in the modern sector can readily confirm, modern medical services are almost never called upon, at least in traditional circles, until African remedies have been exhausted or proven ineffective. In other words, it must be stressed that patients seeking psychiatric hospital care almost always constitute a very specific population, psychologically and sociologically: The psychiatrist is left to salvage the chronic or "incurable" patients. It can be said that hospitalized patients generally tell us more about the failures than about the successes of traditional institutions and forms of therapy — a most important point to which I wish to draw the reader's attention from the outset of this study.

Lastly, if a person is hospitalized, *ipso facto*, he is considered to be *a sick person*. As such, he benefits, so to speak, from a special status on the social and psychosocial planes.

Throughout the discussion to follow (and this is the focus of my own inquiry) the questions raised will bear on the existence, the nature, and the meaning of mental

illness for Africans themselves in a traditional milieu —
for the patient, for the family, for the surrounding
society. If the present study proves to be of any value,
it will be to show how mental illness can be interpreted
(if not analyzed) in terms of traditional anthropological structures.

It seems impossible to get any comprehensive idea of
the conception of mental morbidity, its significance, or
even its frequency and/or the general distribution of
mental disorders in Black Africa from hospital patients
alone. The first problem is the rarity and limited
character of the statistical studies that have been
devoted to the subject; furthermore, in no way do existing studies permit even an approximation of the real
epidemiological incidence of mental illness. In fact, to
my knowledge, they all bear precisely on that narrow
sample consisting of hospital inpatients or outpatients,
for Western-type psychiatric treatment reaches only
those rare persons who are brought by their families or
by competent administrative authority to a dispensary
or hospital. Thus statistical and nosographic investigations touch only a small percentage of the population;
consequently, they are representative neither of patients nor of mental disorders in general.[3]

Collomb (1966) has stated that "the incidence of psychiatric morbidity is at present impossible to estimate.

[3]And immediately, of course, the question one asks is whether the nosographic categories or ranges found in hospitals are the same as those in the
traditional milieu. Or, are not "hospitalizable" (or hospitalized) patients
precisely the persons who happen to correspond, at least in part, to the
nosographic categories characteristic of Western hospitals? Which leads,
of course, to other questions: Who comes to be hospitalized? How? By
whom? Why? (Cf. Storper-Perez, 1968).

. . . No epidemiological survey has been made in Africa, not even a cursory one, and the most fanciful figures are put forward" (p. 423).

Similarly, if one tries to compare mental morbidity in Africa with psychiatric morbidity in the West, the epidemiological results are imprecise, even contradictory. According to most writers, in fact, the frequency of mental illness is lower in Africa than in Western countries: three to six cases per 10,000 as compared with 40 to 50, according to Tooth and Carothers (cited in Collomb, 1966, p. 423; see also Tooth, 1950, and Carothers, 1953). Actually, these frequencies are questionable as they correspond in part only to the semirural population; in certain towns, at least, the rate is very likely higher. Yet what about the rural environment, which in Africa accounts for at least 80 % of the total population?

In a study made in Ethiopia, Giel (1968) estimates that the frequency of mental illness and personality disorder is no less elevated in traditional and rural settings than it is in urban environments.

The same author, in a paper written in collaboration with Van Luijk (Giel and Van Luijk, n.d.), reports the results of an epidemiological investigation bearing on a population of outpatients in the following facilities: a general hospital in Addis Ababa, a police force hospital, a provincial hospital, and a dispensary in a remote community (a bush dispensary). A study of 100 families in a bush district and 100 families in a rural region completes this work, which in all bears on 3,200 persons (sick and not sick). Over a one-year period, 148 persons out of 1,000 sought treatment for psychiatric problems;

however, the authors stress that these figures should be regarded with great caution. In reviewing the literature, Shepherd, Cooper, Brown, and Kalton (1967) have found figures to vary from 4½ % to 6 %.

However, Giel and Van Luijk, comparing psychiatric epidemiology with the epidemiology of infectious disease, report the following findings:

•At Addis Ababa, psychiatric morbidity among hospital outpatients was 18.5% versus 9.5% for infectious diseases.

•At the provincial hospital of Kafa, psychiatric morbidity was 7% versus 28.7% for serious somatic illness (the socioeconomic level being generally low among these patients, who were suffering from severe malnutrition).

•Among the rural patients visiting the bush dispensary, psychiatric morbidity was astonishingly high: 19.5% versus 17.5% for infectious disease.

•At the police force hospital, the psychiatric morbidity was 16.1% versus 9.5% for infectious disease.

The authors call attention to certain nosographic, psychopathological, and clinical aspects of psychiatric morbidity in Ethiopia. They point out, for instance, that somatic complaints are a sanctioned mode of expression and that it is often hard to speak of delusions in connection with certain modes of expression that seem to be an extension of cultural representations. Psychosis, thought to be rare, seems to have a special status; psychotics are tolerated with great patience by the community and are placed in confinement only when their behavior becomes overly aggressive.

The authors stress the quality of the therapeutic relationship and the availability of the therapists, factors that in large measure determine whether psychiatric treatment is sought. A climate characterized by personal contact between the population and the medical staff permits true prophylaxis by preventing a situation in which patients do not come or come too late for consultation.

In conclusion, Giel and Van Luijk contend that mental disorders are undoubtedly as frequent in Ethiopia as they are in countries that are more highly developed from the socioeconomic point of view, such as Great Britain. Stresses — which differ, of course, from those that people have to face in industrialized countries — exist in even the smallest village. Therefore, according to these writers, the fundamental difference does not have to do with the statistical frequency of mental illness but, rather, with the apparently greater coherence and efficacy of African social structures and institutions with regard to the mentally ill.

The investigations of Baker (1959) in Nyasaland (Malawi) reveal that the incidence of mental illness, estimated from the number of hospital admissions in 1958, was a little higher than two cases per 10,000 inhabitants (2/10,000), with the incidence for individual districts ranging from 0.2/10,000 in the district of Karouga, in the far north of the country, to 6.5/10,000 in the district of Zomba. It would appear that the factor that has the greatest influence on the rate of admissions is the accessibility of a modern hospital; for example, more than half of the admissions in Zomba come from the area where the hospital is located. In the regions or zones neighboring the hospital, the rate of admissions varies in inverse proportion to the distance from the hospital, falling to 1.6/10,000 in the most distant area, about 70 miles away.

TABLE 1

Classification of Mental Illness at the Psychiatric Hospital of Zomba

Classification	Hospitalized		Nonhospitalized	
	M	F	M	F
Schizophrenic disturbances	223	129	18	5
Manic-depressive and involutional psychoses	14	26	1	1
Senile and presenile psychoses	10	10	2	—
Cerebral arteriosclerosis	21	9	2	—
Other symptomatic psychoses	36	6	5	—
Anxiety and phobias	7	1	3	—
Hysteria	2	1	—	—
Depressive reactions	7	3	3	6
Other reactive and psychoneurotic states	5	—	3	—
Pathological personality and immaturity	1	—	5	—
Alcoholism and drug dependence	3	—	1	—
Mental deficiencies	4	—	—	1
Epilepsy	60	13	104	57
TOTAL	393	198	147	70

After Baker (1959).

Baker presents (Table 1) the statistics gathered at the psychiatric hospital of Zomba (280 beds) for the year 1958, according to the international classification of mental illness. He stresses the genuinely therapeutic character of the hospital facility, in which priority was given not to *security* but to *treatment*. The results amply vindicated this approach, for the author reports that in two years there had been no case of destructive or aggressive behavior that might have justified isolation of a patient. Also, instead of resorting to "the costly architectural features of an asylum" (1959, p. 2), Baker recommends building small therapeutic units attached to district hospitals.[4] Such a policy would permit more money to be devoted to the training of professional personnel.

Among the clinical manifestations, the most pronounced forms of depression were recognized more frequently than other symptomatic conditions, with an incidence of 8 % in 590 consecutive admissions. Mania, of typical development, was extremely rare (if not nonexistent), with only three cases observed in the same population of 590 patients.

As a rule, the acute manifestations were not very long-lasting. "One finds," writes Baker (1959), "that African rural society is very tolerant regarding aggressive or destructive attitudes, provided that such periods are brief and no great damage is done" (p. 4).

Lastly, Baker calls attention to one point in particular: the high correlation (.75) between admissions and marital disputes. "One can assume that the numerous causes that set man against wife, subject to native law and custom, are a proximate measure of the factors influencing social stability and personal relations, and that similar factors will influence mental health."

Generally speaking, it must be said that hospital statistics, the only data available, provide only a very incomplete picture of the overall psychiatric morbidity

---

[4]This novel idea had already been suggested and put into practice by Father T. A. Lambo, who founded the first supervised therapeutic villages in Nigeria. It should be noted that since that time this system has gained wide acceptance. (See Lambo, 1961, and Woodbury, 1966.)

of a given population. It should be added that the very idea of "mental illness" is especially hard to define in a different culture; instead, we can get a more accurate reading of the threshold of tolerance of a particular population with respect to mental disturbance. In any event, it is important to note that, to date, psychic disorders still represent a very minor public health problem in Africa as compared to the other major pathological categories of medicine (infectious disease, parasitic disease, the principal endemic diseases, etc.).

In view of the present state of psychiatric services in Africa, it is impossible to estimate the number of persons who are mentally ill but who stay at home and avail themselves of care in the traditional manner. The few psychiatrists who work in Africa are for the most part Western psychiatrists or psychiatrists trained in Western universities and the demand for their services is continually growing in certain large towns where they do exist. The number of new patients rose from 500 to 5,000 per year at the neuropsychiatric clinic of Fann during the period from 1959 to 1965.[5]

Still, it is understandable that, in the large urban centers of Africa, the deterioration of traditional frames of reference and ties (whereby everyone's place is fixed in a coherent and structured relational whole) very likely increases the risk of mental disorders. It is even more easily understandable when one considers that well-

[5]See Collomb, 1965a. One may ask, however, whether the halo surrounding the person of Father Collomb does not constitute a systematic bias. At any rate, there was a similar phenomenon at Ibadan concerning Father Lambo, the Nigerian: according to a number of informants, the demand for services fell off considerably after the latter became an official of the World Health Organization at Geneva.

defined relational structures are frequently replaced, at least in the towns, by an amalgam of transplanted populations in the throes of urbanization and ill-prepared for this new way of life. One of the consequences, and not the least of them, is loneliness and a feeling of abandonment.[6]

However that may be, and contrary to so much that has been written on the problem of acculturation, I believe that African societies are, and have been for centuries (some of them for more than a millenium, particularly those of the Sahel), societies in transition, clearly historical. Consequently, the dimension of conflict, in its broader sense, has never been absent. It seems to me the crucial point is that, through the many political and historical changes described by the historians of Africa, a number of cultural features have survived or been adapted giving the African way of life, the pedagogical system, the world view, in short, all the anthropological dimensions of Africa, an undeniably unique and original character.

For proof one need look no further than the intercultural contacts that have taken place historically and, varying with the case, have brought forth new realities while preserving the realities from a far distant past: in

---

[6]Although we must not exaggerate the importance of these new findings, one does in fact note that (a) individuals in large towns tend to group themselves along ethnic lines as well as according to the customary basic patterns of kinship and alliance; (b) traditional therapeutic sessions are actually held far more frequently in the towns and on their outskirts than they are in the country, and in town they play a broader and more *active* functional role in restructuration; and (c) there is indeed a high concentration (corresponding to the demand) of traditional practitioners in the modern cities, which is increasing with urban expansion. These things are readily observed.

other words, change has not always been synonymous with destruction. Furthermore, we can consider the still vital and contemporary character of African culture and religions that were transported three or four centuries ago to the Americas, especially Brazil, Cuba, and the Antilles (Bastide, 1960b; see also Bastide, 1956 and 1960a). Christianity has not succeeded in absorbing them; on the contrary, many followers have been converted among white populations that were originally Catholic.

In a more general way, I believe, along with Mercier (1966, pp. 205–210; see also Balandier, 1955, and Gluckman, 1955), that "conflict" is the raw material of social cohesion, at least in African societies. Conflict does not systematically destroy the social system; on the contrary, the latter accommodates it, acquiring ever-renewed vigor. Groups and individuals, depending on the sector of cultural and social life in question, do not always have the same partners in conflict relationships. Also, conflict does not result in completely rupturing social unity; it only disturbs it, and more or less institutionalized solutions, as the case may be, always intervene. Relations of cooperation and relations of conflict form interlocking networks, the one as important as the other for maintaining the social system.

It is in this frame of reference, I believe, that we must try to understand the therapeutic techniques and other traditional procedures for formalizing and resolving conflicts. These techniques and procedures are interesting in that, drawn from the oldest traditions, they in effect make it possible to resolve contemporary problems, which clearly proves a certain degree of permanence despite historical discontinuity. One should perhaps not hold too creationist a view of culture; a culture grows and evolves while at the same time keeping its own peculiar anthropological and symbolic characteristics.

Consequently, if we are to recapitulate mental illness in language that comes closer to the truth of its structure, then mental illness *qua* conflict, conforming to the traditional representation, should fit into African thinking about disease (with respect to nosology).

Having made that point, if nevertheless we try to classify mental disorders in Africa in terms of the usual international nosographic categories, we find extremely variable percentages for a given population, depending on the period and the psychiatrist reporting. For example, Collomb (1966) notes that the incidence of schizophrenia varies from 15% to 70% for hospital populations of the same type.

In a study bearing on 2,000 patients hospitalized in the psychiatric facility of Fann at Dakar between 1959 and 1965, Collomb (1965a) obtained the results that are presented in Table 2, along with the corresponding proportions according to the standard French and international classifications, taken from Ey (1958).

A comparison of the three parts of the table immediately reveals the remarkable frequency of acute psychoses compared to the chronic forms, and the low representation of neuroses in Africa.

To my knowledge, very few studies with any claim to being systematic (except perhaps for a few monographs) have been devoted to neuroses in Africa. We lack an organized general theoretical framework that might

TABLE 2

Comparison of African with Current Standard French and International Classifications of Mental Illness

African Classification (Senegalese Experience)*							
C	M	D	BD	CD	SCH	N	OP
5%	5%	15%	30%	5%	15%	5%	20%

Current Standard French Classification**						
C	M/D	BD	CD	SCH	N	OP
5%	20%	5%	15%	20%	15%	20%

Current Standard International Classification**				
C	M/D	SCH	N	OP
5%	20%	35%	20%	20%

C, confusional states; M/D, manic states, depressive states, periodic psychoses; BD, bouffées délirantes (transitory delusional states); CD, chronic delirium; SCH, schizophrenia; N, neuroses; OP, organic psychoses.
*After Collomb (1965a).
**After Ey (1958).

make the various manifestations of mental illness in Black Africa intelligible to us. The elements of such a general theory (if possible) can be formulated, in my opinion, only in terms of African anthropological structures themselves.

Meanwhile, it should be noted that in the context of modern institutional practice, in contrast to the rarity of systematized neuroses of the obsessional or phobic type, clinical descriptions record a high frequency of states of anxiety—"an almost normal component of the sociocultural situation" (Lambo cited in Collomb, 1966, p. 426)—with hysteria, or what could be called that according to Western concepts, representing the most frequent neurotic organization in the view of a number of writers.

It is exceptional to come across obsessional psychoneuroses, especially those forms observed in the West. In light of what we know about traditional upbringing and the growth and development of the personality in Africa, this rarity of obsessional neuroses does not surprise psychoanalysts who have taken an interest in the phenomenon. To use the terms of the analytical view (if that view is valid), this infrequency becomes completely understandable when one considers the unobtrusiveness of the anal component and the absence of rigid defensive organizations in the development of the personality.[7]

As for phobic behaviors, they usually seem to be "imposed" by general outside circumstances. In any case, the phobogenic object is often diffuse and is always related to symbols whose cultural meaning is plain or can easily be analyzed in that respect. Moreover, phobias are centered almost exclusively on situations or places associated with the presence of malevolent beings (spirits, sorcerers, etc.), in whose existence the whole community believes. The phobogenic object is never an object of "absurd" fantasy, in terms of being purely narcissistic and hard to "put into words." To my way of

---

[7]In my own analyses, I shall try to show that, in a more general way, the extreme rarity of neuroses organized along Western lines (psychoneuroses) is due much more directly to the relatively open structure of the personality in traditional Africa, whereas morbid structures (in particular obsessional neurosis, melancholic psychosis, and paranoid psychosis) unquestionably imply, from the point of view of a comprehensive dynamic psychology: (a) a closed personality structure (complete internality of the subject), (b) total internalization of the conflict that is at the root of the morbid structure, and (c) a sociocultural context of sin and guilt, with all three features, of course, being complementary and mutually reinforcing. Similarly, a psychoanalytical interpretation, if it pretends to be rigorous, assumes the same threefold condition.

thinking, a "fantasized" object phobia implies a closed personality structure, which makes it possible to capture, enclose, and appropriate the object for personal ends. To defend its internal coherence, therefore, a closed structure may construct a fortuitous fantasy object (displacement) of benign self-terrorism from the outside (the individualized persecutory phobogenic object), *less* threatening to internal equilibrium, which it *alone* is capable of protecting. Generally, however, in Africa the best defenses are mainly, if not exclusively, socialized group defenses, which are found in the vast reservoir of the structured collective imaginary.

Similarly, care should be taken not to immediately liken states of anxiety to anxiety neurosis in connection with all the states of concern that are so easily triggered by some unexpected event, a change in circumstances, a rupture or shift in relations with others, some personal problem, the breach of a taboo. The idea of neurosis, in the Western sense, or anxiety neurosis, implies a personality characterized by a permanent neurotic structure (Collomb, 1965a). In Africa, the states of anxiety in question are accompanied by numerous and varied somatic manifestations expressed with great intensity; acute attacks of anxiety are often felt and described as being caught in the grip of "sorcery," an experience marked by a keen sense of imminent death.

Acting "hysterical," at least as a descriptive clinical category, is considered by virtually all writers to be the most characteristic form of neurotic expression in Africa. "Hysteria is the hall-mark of psychiatry in Africans. . . . The hysterical mechanism is so readily employed that conversion symptoms colour not only neurotic depressions and anxiety states but also true psychoses" (Dembovitz, cited in Carothers, 1953, p. 150).

This position should be qualified, however, for the tendency to seek expression through somatic complaints, widespread as it may be, in no way justifies our identifying every somatization with hysterical conversion. "One must distinguish, on the one hand, hysterical symptoms, which have the quality of a message, coming out of the unconscious through a symbolic chain, and, on the other hand, the more or less violent and spectacular somatic manifestations that accompany any emotional state" (Collomb, 1965a, p. 46).

It is important, then, to make a distinction between, at one level, the *expression* of being sick, which is manifested through the body (with the body always participating), and, at another level, the *meaning* of the message "spoken" by the body.

Throughout this book we shall be examining in greater detail the theoretical framework in which the problem of expression and meaning can be analyzed, without having to call upon concepts that are alien to cultural meanings of the traditional African world. We shall experience a certain discomfort, however, in trying to transpose—if only in terms of descriptive nosographic categories—phenomena reported with reference to Western hysteria, knowing in all honesty that hysteria, as such, implies a whole theory, explicit or implicit, concerning the structuration of the personality.

Notwithstanding, in this chapter I shall continue to review "nosographic" studies or inquiries that have been carried out in the field, using the same terminology in which they are reported. However, I cannot refrain from stressing from the start that it would be "pushing things too far" to try to understand the problem of the expression and meaning of the *message* (a hysterical message?) in terms of the Freudian ontogeny of stages or any other genetic theory that does not take into account the structuration of the African person/personality.

It seems quite obvious to me that if we truly want to understand the meaning of a message, any message, we must still first figure out the code. The fact of the matter is, as I shall attempt to show, this code cannot be deciphered with any accuracy except within the structures of traditional thought, not in terms of some dogma that is extraneous to it. In other words, the theoretical problem that confronts us, already at the level of the symptom itself, is that of finding out what it is a symptom of. And that problem is what makes any nosography suspect; there can be no strictly "innocent" nosography, that is, one that does not rest in turn on a nosology. A coherent nosology, however, implies a theoretical approach to the psychology of behavior. And I fail to see how there could really be meaningful forms of behavior that are not well-defined social structures; otherwise, "speaking" would not be "saying" anything.

With respect to the problem of the psychoses, a question arises concerning the application of international nosography to African psychopathology: namely, whether the distinction between neuroses and psychoses remains fully valid in a traditional milieu. Numerous writers, Collomb in particular, have called attention to the fact that it is often difficult to distinguish neurotic from psychotic states, so common are delusional manifestations (or at any rate delusion as it is defined in the

West), which may occur with the slightest psychological or physical malaise. Even the boundaries of delusion are not always easy to perceive, a point we shall come back to later.

If we continue, however, to use the international classification for analyzing African clinical data, we can pose the question of the relative frequency of acute and chronic psychoses. Although the various authors are not in complete agreement on this point, a number of characteristics nevertheless emerge.

First of all, the frequency of the different psychoses varies considerably according to the statistics. For example, the percentage of schizophrenics among hospitalized patients ranges from 6.98% to 56.7%, with an average of 15%, for countries using the international classification. This rate of 15% for schizophrenia is found in the hospital population of Dakar, as compared with 30% for *bouffées délirantes* or transitory delusional states (Ayats, 1968).

Lambo considers schizophrenia[8] to be the most commonly encountered chronic mental illness in Africans between the ages of 16 and 49 years. In his opinion, its growing incidence is related to the magnitude of the social changes that are taking place. The figures pre-

---

[8]In regard to Lambo, as well as a number of other authors writing in English, the reader should bear in mind that in English "schizophrenia" covers a very wide field, including not only acute psychotic outbursts but also certain systematized forms of delusion, which the French school would place instead under the headings of chronic hallucinatory psychosis, paraphrenia, and polymorphous *bouffées délirantes*, as distinguished from forms of schizophrenia proper. Consequently, it is not clear whether what is called schizophrenia in Dakar (Collomb) involves the same clinical reality that is classified under that heading in Ibadan, Abeokuta, and Dar es Salaam.

sented are, as we have seen, highly variable; it is clearly not an easy matter to reach agreement on the clinical reality that encompasses schizophrenia, especially in African societies. For instance, Collomb (1965a, p. 51) cites Moffson (1955) reporting 56.7% and Lamont and Blignault (1953) reporting 55.8% for the incidence of schizophrenia among psychiatric admissions in South Africa, whereas Baasher (1961) reports a rate of only 6.98% for schizophrenia in the Sudan.

At Faan (Dakar) the rate remains stable from one year to the next at approximately 15%, a rate lower than that indicated in the international classification (35%) and also lower than that in the French classification (20%).

Major paranoid delusions are rare and are observed mainly in persons who have been in contact with Western culture. As a rule, the rarity of catatonic forms is cited, along with the frequency of simple forms (Collomb, 1966).

It seems clear, at the nosographic level, that somatization and symptoms of a hysterical type are commonly observed in numerous psychotics. Lambo (1968), in comparing an unschooled rural group and a schooled urban group, found that somatic complaints and hypochondriacal themes predominated in the second group, whereas the first group was more likely to seek expression in a delusional mode, with themes directly related to collective magicoreligious representations and to the ancestor cult.

The development of schizophrenia in an African milieu differs from the classical description of international nosography. Lambo (1968) has compared the long-term evolution of psychosis in a Westernized group with its evolution in a rural group: the developmental and diagnostic criteria are completely comparable in Westerners and in Africans who have had close contact with Western culture. In contrast, in the traditional rural group, the symptoms are more polymorphous and the prognosis is better.

Chronicity is generally less pronounced in Africa than it is in the West. This difference seems to be due mainly to great tolerance on the part of the community, which facilitates rapid reintegration into the family group, as well as to the quality of human relationships.

Asuni (1968) draws similar conclusions from his investigation of the histories of certain vagrant psychotics, who are particularly numerous in the town of Abeokuta. These persons, all classified as schizophrenics and whose illness dates back several years, prefer to frequent the bustling, populous quarters of town (markets, stations, etc.) rather than the less lively residential areas. The quest for contact with the social group is also expressed by the way these vagrants wander about in the midst of crowds, whereas depressed patients seek refuge in the most deserted areas. At the same time, Asuni is struck by the absence of symptoms that are regularly found in patients who have been hospitalized for long periods in Western surroundings, such as lack of pragmatism and profound disinterest.

Like other writers, Asuni notes that rejection of the mentally ill becomes more common and more emphatic as the environment becomes more urbanized.

I share the view of Haworth (1968) who warns against

the tendency to be too hasty in applying the label schizophrenic to what one takes to be a communication disorder, a disturbance of the thought process, but what in fact can be truly understood and interpreted only in light of the cultural context from which it cannot be arbitrarily separated. Haworth goes on to raise the problems of hallucination and delusion, the meanings of which are often transparent — phenomena that in many cases appear to be consistent with the collective representations normally employed by the group.

It is not always easy to draw the line between mythic-poetic language and "alienated" speech. Haworth thinks that the term schizophrenic is erroneously applied to cases that can, in reality, be seen as *comprehensible* acute reactive psychoses. In effect, the psychotic episode constitutes an original element, specific to African psychiatry, illustrating in particularly clear fashion the importance of the idea of persecution in all representation.[9]

Bouffées délirantes are a characteristic feature of African psychiatry, not only in the traditional, rural environment but also in the towns and among transplanted Africans (similar observations have been made among the blacks in Cuba by Bustamente).

From a study of 125 cases observed at Fann (Dakar) over a period of 14 months, Collomb (1965b) estimates that the incidence of such episodes, compared to other

[9]That is why, throughout this study, in the realm of research I have questioned the value of a "universal" nosography, stripped of all prior psychological and psychopathological knowledge. In other words, we may ask, if nosography makes it possible to define a field at a superficial level, what is it really all about at a deeper level?

so-called "functional" psychoses, is about 30 %. This figure is relatively high if one looks at the much debated and in any case low ranking of transitory delusional states in Western psychiatry (5% among all psychoses and serious neuroses, according to Collomb, 1965a).[10]

Psychotic episodes, notable for their sudden, explosive character and their tendency not to become chronic, are more likely to occur when there is some change in relations or in the environment, that is, when a person is called upon, owing to outside pressures, to play a part other than his usual part (Collomb, 1965b). According to Collomb, delusional outbursts seem to derive from a difficult situation that throws into question a person's role, his very being for others.

Collomb suggests that the importance of the social and family group in the structuring of the personality (with the person representing the deeper layer, and the persona, the superficial layer) and the precise, even rigid, definition of everyone's role and rank within that group may account for the readiness with which a crisis erupts when social changes or ruptures occur. The emergence of new values and of roles hitherto unknown in developing societies is a source of anxiety and confusion.[11] Thus acute psychotic attacks are becoming increasingly frequent, especially in urban areas.

[10]Simple nosography is quite incapable of answering important questions such as why chronic psychosis in the Nordic countries tend toward encystment. Similarly, one may wonder, for example, about the significance of the problem of defilement, the pure and the impure, an issue that dominates Swedish psychopathology.

[11]This point, of fundamental theoretical importance, was discussed at length in *Psychiatrie dynamique africaine* (I. Sow, 1977). In my opinion, the acute psychotic outbursts elicited at certain stages of initiation, and

The usually favorable outcome of *bouffée délirante* clearly indicates that the delusional episode does not consummate a rupture with the group; the relationship to others remains quite open. Under normal traditional conditions, the group works not to exclude but to reintegrate the disturbed person into the community.

Since everything that happens gives evidence of some temporary problem in the dynamics of the patient's normal relations, it suffices to discover and then clarify the etiology of the problem (diagnosing the troublesome relational structure) to determine the therapeutic action to be taken. To my way of thinking, delusion is not, like an object, some morbid outgrowth; rather it is like the living flesh of personal existence as one of the major expressions of the essence of life. Delirium verbalizes the pathetic relationship of one being with another; by the same token, it enables us to perceive, beneath the surface, the symbolic structures that order this pathetic verbalization. Moreover, we find that delusional episodes are less alienating for the person affected as long as they remain available and accessible to him as a mode of existence. As Collomb (1965b) points out, delirium "is excused and given consideration on the part of others; it still constitutes dialogue and does not isolate the individual by alienating him" (p. 229).

We can better understand how certain Western writers may speak of Africans' real familiarity with hallucinatory experience in essentially normal cir-

---

also induced during the training of certain therapists and the like, correspond more to a complete overthrow and refashioning of the personality; in their impact, then, they go far beyond the confines of rank and role.

cumstances. And we also know that there are numerous techniques for breaking through the guard of the conscious to let the deeper layers of the psychic system speak out (cf. I. Sow, 1977, chaps. 2 and 3).

In the same vein, Collomb (1965b) and his colleagues at Fann have endeavored to show how certain forms of delirium are "socialized into behaviors that have a function of regulation and prevention" (pp. 235–236). In their opinion, the rarity of the schizophrenic development in the strict sense is related to the way in which delusional experience is accepted by the group: "Familiarity with delusional experience... characterizes the attitude not only of the disturbed person but of those around him as well" (p. 184).

In the traditional world, delirium is not a strange, incomprehensible phenomenon; it is part of life and, as such, it always has some explanation. "The beneficial consequences of this attitude, which brings neither rejection nor alienation, are evident. The rapid resolution of delusional episodes without their becoming chronic is often the rule" (Collomb, 1965b, p. 185). According to Collomb's statistics, 90% of the patients were cured quickly, 4.5% could not be followed up, and 5.5% showed no perceptible improvement after several weeks of hospitalization.

Collomb maintains that in African cultures, the person, that is, the deeper layer of the personality, is formed in a fusional relationship, being organized without anxiety or early prohibitions. Splitting, then, would come after communication, if one shares Collomb's view of the transitory delusional state as a kind of disorder of communication or narration, whereas

schizophrenia is a disturbance of the unity that antedates narration and, in a way, prohibition.

If the psychotic episode is characteristic as to form,
persecution is unquestionably the theme that is most frequently encountered and most significant in all African
psychiatry. The idea of persecution occupies a prominent position in the anthropological system of representations in Black Africa. In regard to what concerns us
here, it should be noted that this idea of persecution col-
ors the whole of African psychiatry. Invoked by the patient, it is taken up by the family and community, given
form and utilized by the traditional therapist. It constitutes, therefore, a socialized, intracommunity defense,
firmly institutionalized and most effective.

At the deepest levels of the sociocultural universe,
persecution as a theme suggests that the coherence of
anyone's personal structure may be disturbed by an outside force or "externality" if it attacks what constitutes
the foundation of individual existence: the equilibrium
of the complex of constituent relations that go to make
up the self (see I. Sow, 1977). That means that the importance of the idea of persecution can be fully appreciated only by examining the traditional anthropological structures themselves. Only then will we be
able to understand how and why the idea of persecution
functions as a veritable institution that defends both the
individual and the community by giving them a certain
coherence (a fundamental point discussed at length in I.
Sow, 1977).

Thus a living person (in his physical, mental, or social
substance) is thought to be subject to destructive attacks
from certain spirits or individuals (themes about the

powers of sorcerers, marabouts, or fetishers, for example). It is understandable, then, that mental illness may be experienced as persecution in an immediate and fundamental way, in that it undermines a person's normal equilibrium by loosing him from his normal ties and thereby disrupts the community order. In all traditional cultures "the world is ordered, stable, and always meaningful" (M. Diop et al., 1964, p. 340). Persecution becomes "the explanation for everything that disturbs order, disrupts relations, attacks the individual in his physical, mental, or social being" (M. Diop et al., 1964, p. 333).

In other words, as a theme with two poles, since it intensifies existential experience and, at the same time, fixes and thereby moderates the individual's anxiety, persecution is always present in the traditional world. However, as soon as one leaves the fold of these highly cohesive African cultural communities, this institutional system — as an effective socialized defense — becomes more risky, precisely because these reassuring cultural frames of reference disappear more or less completely. This gives way, for example, to some general interpsychological system in which the main valid and valued defenses (which one learns at a very early age) consist in purely individual defenses.

In terms of evidence, quasiexperimental, one may cite the peculiar and well-known onset of delusional psychotic episodes (see, in particular, M. Diop, 1968). In certain situations of insecurity (often associated on the psychological level with positive attempts to reorganize defenses), as real-life troubles abate, psychotic episodes of "readjustment" sometimes occur in transplanted African students or trainees. It is highly significant, moreover, to find that at the time of these psychotic decompensations, the thematic content of the delusions, save for negligible elements of formulation, is at first identical to what one observes in patients living in traditional surroundings. Beyond all question, there are common fundamental structures, even, and indeed especially, in having delusions. Later, as the case evolves (when the development is favorable), there emerges in the new theme — reconstructing the personality — a selective integration of certain elements of the host culture in the form of a conflict having a persecutory structure, which will gradually become conventional.

Be that as it may, the psychiatric problem in present-day Black Africa does not appear to be an alarming medical, medicopsychological, or medicosocial problem, as seems to be the case (according to the World Health Organization) in certain Western countries. The principal endemic contagious diseases, the various parasitic diseases, hygiene, children's diseases, major surgery, etc., present the most urgent problems and, for this very reason, command most of the attention of local public health authorities.

The social incidence of mental illness seems, to me at any rate, quite minimal. One can testify to this despite the lack of valid statistical data.[12] One of the most frequently advanced hypotheses points to the fact that tra-

[12]While writing this book, I found that the World Health Organization itself did not have valid or reliable comprehensive official statistics regarding the incidence or distribution of psychiatric disorders in Black Africa (not even in the modern hospital sector, much less in the traditional sector).

ditional institutions, for the most part, still remain efficacious both in their preventive function and in their
prophylactic function of maintaining personal, interpersonal, and community equilibrium. Factors that are
often cited are:

•a broad family canopy, positive and effective in
almost all cases;

•a very great tolerance on the part of others, along
with a structure of community life and an unusual conception of illness in general;

•effective psychological — in fact, cultural — defenses, such as the externalization of conflict, with
precise group identification of a persecutor, and the
protected status of the patient, as a victim whom the
group gathers round.

Contrary to what some writers say, the essential
truth, beyond certain appearances of modernity, which
can be deceptive on superficial observation, is that daily
social relations at all levels of African society are in fact
dominated by the great legacy of traditional cultural
values. One comes to appreciate this fully when personal crises occur or when important decisions must be
made concerning life, politics, and other vital matters,
for, as everywhere, only in such circumstances does the
true structure of an individual emerge. To be concrete, I
firmly believe that in Africa today no one (chiefs of
state, politicians, technocrats, and modern intel-
lectuals included) can, in his everyday social practice,
remove himself — other than verbally — from the essence
of traditional structures: the precedence linked to
seniority and the rules of respect; the psychology and
psychosociology, as it were, of "shame"; the sharing in

privileged relationships and the forming of family bonds in major ceremonies concerning birth (baptism), union (marriage), and death (mourning); and so on.

For a long time to come, daily life will undoubtedly be marked by the imprint of traditional culture. And we know that mental structures always survive long beyond real-life social, economic, and political changes. Consequently, there can be no simple, automatic interaction between the two domains; instead, there are complex relations of a dialectical nature, the evolution of which — and this is the least that could be said — constitutes, at a certain level, the living history of every people.

By and large, with respect to individual dynamics, a hypothesis can be accepted that the idea of guilt is the core of psychopathology and the foundation of any school of Western psychiatry that purports to be comprehensive. Indeed, this dynamic concept of guilt lies at the very center of not only the theory but also the treatment of the principal Western forms of morbid organization. It can even be said that Western clinical psychology and psychopathology have formulated coherent theories solely from views that place this notion of guilt at the center of individual dynamics.

In the African world, however, in the realm of clinical expression, ideas of guilt and unworthiness do not form the central dynamic elements that explain the development of psychopathological behavior. On the contrary, what underlies such behavior, in a latent fashion in this case, are the dynamics of persecution. Remarkably clear and striking, persecution is a well-known feature in the field of African psychological, psycho-

social, and psychiatric experience. The idea of transgression (sin) and the more or less latent guilt that may
be attached thereto are never expressed with the intensity and conviction that are usually found in typical
melancholic depression, for example, or that are interpreted as pregenital anxiety (oral or anal), or as oedipal
guilt, a constant of the innermost structure of all the
neuroses examined or treated by Western clinicians.

In African psychopathology, the most frequent
themes during actual attacks of depression are themes of
persecution: the individual feels depressed from the outside, by the outside. The threat comes from without and
not from some internalized force. As Collomb and
Zwingelstein (1962) point out, "value is bestowed by the
social group and not by an internalized individual
superego" (p. 524).

It is interesting to find the close link that exists between feelings of depression and of persecution in the
thematic repertory of African patients. Whereas the depressive state might not be identified, persecution can
always be more readily recognized. On the practical
level, that approach would seem to offer better therapeutic possibilities.

In the view of Prince (1962) of Nigeria, depression is
one of the most common syndromes in Africa, if included in depression are somatic complaints and depressive
equivalents. If, on the contrary, depression is confined
to typical melancholic depression, it proves to be extremely rare if not nonexistent (Collomb, 1965a).

Whatever may be the reality of manic-depressive psychosis in other respects — and it is seen very differently
depending on the writer — its least debatable feature is

the markedly lower frequency of melancholic forms compared to manic forms (let us say, more cautiously, psychotic-like states of depression versus psychotic-like states of excitement). Carothers (cited by M. Diop, 1961; see Carothers, 1947 and 1951), in comparing the figures obtained for Africans and Europeans, respectively, who were admitted to the same hospital during the same period (1939-1948), found 24 cases of depression out of 1,508 African patients or only 1.6%, whereas the corresponding rate for the 222 European patients was 22%.

In any event, persecution almost always appears as a primary phenomenon, which again brings us back to the problem of the etiological externality of these disorders and, as a consequence, to the absence of self-blame or guilt, with a corresponding absence of self-aggressiveness — indeed, the extreme rarity of suicides is a striking feature of African psychiatry.

The date collected, both in hospital settings and from systematic inquiries in urban and rural surroundings, confirm the very low frequency of suicide in Africa: D. Sow (1962) reports .78 per 100,000 inhabitants for Senegal, and Asuni (1961), less than one per 100,000 for Nigeria, the average rate for Europe and the United States being 17 per 100,000. M. Diop (1961) notes that suicide is most exceptional for African women, although depression is extremely frequent among the female population (being expressed in a variety of clinical modalities, but with a sense of persecution always present).

According to all observers, then, the most fundamental feature to emerge from an overall view of African psychiatric practice is clearly the importance of the idea of conflict and the significance of persecution, aspects that raise the crucial question of externality and internality in mental illness. Luc de Heusch (1971) has caught perfectly the conception of mental illness as persecution in the following passage: "The sickness, which must be got rid of, or, rather, which must be brought under control, is thought of as a force of witchcraft, that is, as a form of aggression from the outside world that alters the psychic personality" (p. 237).

To be understandable, the rarity, even the absence, of paranoid and melancholic psychoses and obsessional neuroses must be related to the organization of the person/personality in African culture. Those clinical entities, highly personalized in international nosography, reflect a maximal internalization of the persecutory agency. To describe it one way, behavior prohibitions are set up for the African child relatively late (after the age of six), and it is hard to speak of the internalized and personalized judicial agency (superego); moral authority, though omnipresent, remains *outside* the individual as such. In Western culture, on the contrary, the deliberate teaching of internalization of law and, consequently, of guilt plays a fundamental role in development of the personality, so that at the psychological and psychopathological levels, the source of sickness is to be sought in the sick person himself. In Africa, however, threats and persecution can come only from without: any member of the community, if he breaks the prohibitions ensuring the cohesion and homogeneity of the group, is likely to become the target of outside forces and hence to fall victim to them (becoming ill or deranged). We can discern here the African conception of mental illness, as well as the African attitude toward sickness and those who are sick, deriving from the organization of the person/personality.

As long as persecution can form a defensive theme that is culturally confirmed in a particular system of social relations, mental illness will be an "affliction" and will always remain understandable to others, being perceived and accepted without the distressing emotional overtones that accompany and/or characterize it in noncohesive, individualistic societies.

Contrary to what one finds in the West, African clinical experience indicates that persecution does not follow directly from guilt through the mechanism of projection. One may go on to suggest that, in all probability, the dynamic conception of guilt is clearly understandable only within the Judeo-Christian anthropological context of sin, with purely personal guilt representing, in the end, the complete internalization of sin.[13]

As I have tried to show elsewhere (I. Sow, 1977), to combat the "disorder" that ushers in madness, traditional society employs specific therapeutic techniques, based on precise etiological concepts, drawn from nosological outlines that are themselves derived from the African idea of the personality and its vicissitudes. Never, in the traditional world, is treatment reduced to a dual relationship of the sort one finds in the West — prolonged, sometimes interminable, one-to-one conversation; instead, it should lead rather quickly to a

[13]The idea of guilt is so intimately bound up with the individual in the West, that one may ask whether the moral context of sin does not constitute the special breeding ground of psychoneurosis, strictly speaking.

new and necessary equilibrium between the patient and his constituent poles, to a readjustment of relational polarities (the vertical order of tradition, the family, the community). In short, what we are talking about here are the most profound relations of the individual with his constituent elements and with the component sociocultural forces that provide coherence and consistency in a interdependent universe.

Traditional societies are marked by an absence of alienation, in the Western sense of the term (i.e., radical isolation with respect to self and others), a phenomenon that should be related, in all likelihood, to the absence of any radical separation between delusional productions, the cultural themes of the collective imaginary, and the innermost structure of the person/personality. As Ortigues and Ortigues (1966) remark, "delusions of persecution arise from a cultural background in which the persecutory position is the norm, serving to regulate social relations. . . . The hallucinatory phenomena described are, similarly, extensions of common, everyday experiences. For the society, they do not seem pathological per se" (p. 302).

In its deepest reading, madness is a "sign"; it indicates immediately that the person affected is expressing some conflict — a conflict between himself and the external life forces that make up his personality, according to the traditional view. It will be the task of the traditional therapist, with the close cooperation of the community and the family, to interpret the sign, that is, to determine the sector that has become troublesome in the networks that make up the innermost structure of the personality. It is a question of transforming mental disturbance into articulate language, that is, of restoring a shattered order, whose effect is not just personal or individual. Reestablishing order in the afflicted person, or victim, also means reconstructing the broken bond, reintegrating the patient into the place from which he had been shut out, cut off from his constituent life forces by the "aggressor." First of all, then, the illness must be transformed into a system of communication (cf. Heusch, 1971, p. 236), common knowledge that clearly underscores the importance of the idea of structural continuity between the individual's person/personality and the outside life forces that give him his coherence. One finds that with certain practitioners, among the Fon of Dahomey for example, it is not the sick person himself who undergoes treatment (Heusch, 1971, p. 239).

The efficacy of traditional therapeutic methods hinges on group consensus (the fundamental problem — according to Lévi-Strauss, 1958, p. 180 — revolves around the relationship between an individual and the group, or, more precisely, between a certain type of individual and certain expectàtions of the group), for the group regards sickness as an attack on the spiritual essence through the intrusion of a pathogenic agent and sees the healing powers of the sorcerer and group cohesion as the only means of escaping chaos, of escaping "the intolerable, shocking violence done to man" (Heusch, 1971, p. 249).

As I have argued elsewhere at greater length (see I. Sow, 1977, especially chaps. 2 and 3), the line between reality and dreaming is never as sharp as the Western world may think. Waking thought is not purged of its imaginary content, and there are no hard and impenetrable divisions between the various "psycho-logical" productions of the psychic system. A vast and fertile field of study no doubt lies in the analysis of the structure of the imaginary in traditional societies. It may well be, however, that the imaginary and its pro-ductions do not really create a problem except within social structures characterized by excessive (defensive) individualism; in that case, the imaginary becomes fragmented in strictly narcissistic fantasies, posing a direct threat to others, unless, within the closed con-sciousness of each individual, these same fantasies do not represent a fear of aggression from others. It is inter-esting to note that, in societies having a marked individ-ualistic structure, in interpersonal relations there is a return to the "aggressor-victim" pair at the level of the fantasy dialectic, expressing, by and large, at least the waking social relationships of narcissistic competition.

As regards clinical practice and daily social inter-course in traditional societies, dream imagery, hallucinations, mediumistic states of consciousness, etc., take on added value in that traditionally all these productions lead to a meaning having a collective value, at the end of which lies what is culturally signified. The signified lies outside the individual, who merely serves as its vector, which explains, at least in part, the greater tolerance in regard to mental derangement.

For example, the traditional practitioner (who is not a shaman) will attempt to bring to light not the in-dividual and narcissistic aspect of a dream, as con-clusive in itself, but rather the connection of a dream's content to what is culturally signified, beyond the dream itself. Interesting dreams are signs in another form of speech. They maintain a continuity with others — a continued dynamic relationship in dreaming — and ultimately a continuity between man and culture. Dreaming, then, is pursued in a "rational" form of human discourse, which, in the traditional view, could not be simply the language of biological drives. In short, dreams are the nocturnal expression of human relations. They are ever and always cultural in character.

I believe that, at base, the analysis of dreams and other imaginary productions purely in terms of narcissistic instincts or wishes is not completely justified (classically and theoretically) except in societies in which almost irreducible conflicts develop — verging on the permanent — between the (daytime) culture and the (nighttime) countercultural or subversive schemes of individual desire. Looked at in that light, dreams can be viewed as a veritable single-handed challenge to the diurnal structures of social relations. In that sense, certain "Freudian" dreamers are protesters without knowing it.

Traditional treatment, as many writers have pointed out, ensures the coherence of the psychic universe, which is in turn closely bound up with the social universe (Lévi-Strauss, 1958, p. 182). Consequently, it seems to me imperative that from the start we use the signifiers that belong to the patient's general culture. To mark the boundary between what is and what is not pathological, we surely cannot be content simply to call upon the criteria adopted by Western society. In Africa, mental illness and its treatment fall within specific frames of reference, because the basic structure of the individual and the organization of the personality that

flows therefrom have their own cultural characteristics
(see I. Sow, 1977) that differ from what we are familiar
with, practically and theoretically, concerning the concept of person and the organization of personality in the
West. Mental illness is a disorder, to be sure, but that
disorder, perceived as such in all traditional societies, is
thought of and acted on in terms of "order," in an articulated series of significant sequences aimed at
reestablishing communication with the world of the
signified. In this sense, the patient (because of the
disorder of his problems) provides a perfect opportunity
for a diagnosis of the consistency of the community's ties
with fundamental group values. When there is a cure,
recovery can sometimes be looked on as completion of
an initiation, recreating a union between the signified
and the person cured. We shall examine later on the implications that such a union of certain former "sufferers"
with the signified can have.

In the third chapter of this study, we shall see that in
the traditional African view the universe is made up of
three interrelated but hierarchical worlds: the immediate, social, perceptible world (the microcosmos);
the intermediate world of genies, spirits, and all kinds of
benevolent and malevolent forces (the mesocomos); and
the world beyond the senses (of the Chosen Spirits, the
Ancestors, God). We shall see how there develops a
perpetual dialectic of ambivalent relations between the
inhabitants of the mesocosmos and those of the
microcosmos. The dramatic ups and downs that ensue
can — like relational problems — sometimes result in
mental disturbance. We shall see that Africans regard
the mesocosmos as the realm of violent but also
peaceable doubles; it is the seat of aggressive forces but

also of those that gratify everyday wishes. In short, it is a parallel nocturnal world, structured and organized like a replica of the microcosmic diurnal society.

According to the African conception, the mesocosmos is today the place — the collective, exclusive, and permanent site — where conflicts are transposed, develop, and unfold; it is the inexhaustible source of the collective imaginary, which feeds and gives structure to the individual imaginary. It can be readily understood how, depending on the case, mental derangement may appear to men by turns as an illness, as a therapeutic phenomenon, or, in the words of Heusch (1971), as "a continuous field of varying supernatural manifestations" (p. 255). At the theoretical level, a thorough knowledge of the African mesocosmos contains the key to all African psychology, individual and collective. Any profound transformation of the structure of mental attitudes — should it take place — must, of necessity, come about through the transformation of the state of this mesocosmos. Meanwhile, because of the richness of its thematic content, it constitutes one of the most important reservoirs of African culture.

Here, I should like to mention that the efficacy of traditional methods of healing has been brought to light in particular by the many university research groups (at Dakar, Abidjan, Ibadan, Kinshasa, etc.) but also through the work of numerous individuals. To cite only a few, I refer the reader to the studies of Atiwiya (1971), Gravrand (1966), Lebeuf (1958), Pidoux (1954), Rouch (1960), Sangmuah (1968), and Zempleni (1969).

The treatment is always etiological, for any mental affliction has a cause that also has social meaning, and in the traditional view, its discovery alone makes it possible to arrive at a cure, that is, to bring about a resolution of tensions. As I have mentioned, and shall discuss in detail later on, mental illness is an affliction; it is marked by the idea of conflict between the individual and external persecutory forces. Consequently, a link is created between what appears on the surface and what lies deeper, which — especially in states that we can call psychotic — opens the way to a true rebirth both for the patient and for all the members of the community as well. Seen in that light, therapeutic treatment comprehends the total psychological being, restoring psychological integrity but also strengthening the power to survive.

On looking closer, we find the patient is not the only one to be affected by therapeutic order; the benefits are reflected in the cultural order and the relational structure of the entire group. The affliction "which was open to death, the prospect of death . . . is paradoxically enriched by a positive dimension. . . . Illness (and especially psychotic experience) is but a call to reforge the bonds that exist between men and the spirits, and even an election, opening the way to the career of healer or divine. This last case confirms that misfortune is the necessary and sufficient condition for the blossoming of communication with the sacred" (Heusch, 1971, p. 253).

As we shall see, if mental affliction is a sign, the diagnostic process, as well as interpretation, will make it possible to apprehend the specificity of the signified.

Delusional experience does not imply an unbridgeable gap, a radically different view of the world.

The cured patient is looked on as someone to whom something very important has happened and who has managed to triumph in a particularly dangerous trial; he possesses a knowledge acquired through intimate experience. It is exactly as if he had undergone a real initiation — in short, a kind of successful and integrated cultural psychoanalysis.

Thus one comes to understand that in the traditional panstructured universe, the consistent use of cultural signifiers makes delusion a collective signifier.

The elaboration of a traditional nosology — based on indigenous African clinical realities and aimed at coherently organizing concrete psychopathological data — is conceivable, then, not in terms of nosographic categories (clinical pictures) related, after the fact, to a general treatise on mental illness (nosology), but first and foremost in terms of classification by cause and meaning.

From the traditional point of view, cause and meaning are far more important than the symptom per se; such an approach is more synthetic than that of Western clinical methods, which are heirs to an essentially analytical medical tradition. As we can observe in the field, what is of greatest interest to the African patient from the very beginning and above anything else is the cause or, more importantly, the meaning of his illness, since it is felt to be a misfortune — indeed, much more interesting than the syndromic, even significant, pattern of some objective morbid structure that would be extraneous to him. It is his personal drama, experienced by him, that will be the center of his concern, and it will always be on this particular point that he will judge the competence and skills of his therapist.

I thought it essential to bring out in this first introductory chapter, the highly problematical character of any attempt to apply international nosographic categories[14] directly to clinical manifestations observed in Africa. We are forced to seek new criteria in order to define the semiology itself, other than with conceptual categories worked out in terms of quite different semantic axes.

To go to the heart of the matter, the elaboration of an authentic African psychopathology is essential. That field of inquiry is closely and reciprocally related, moreover, to a deeper understanding of the innermost structure of the person/personality, as well as its constituent and component forces, which play, whether willed or not, a determining role both in the genetic development of the ego and in its incorporation of emotional, affective, personal, and interpersonal elements (cf. I. Sow, 1977, chaps. 1 and 2).

In a precise and concrete way, then, the meaning and also the scope of the concept of mental illness in Black Africa turn on the anthropological position of the individual and the structure of the personality in African society. That is why the simple application of nosological categories that pay no heed either to the psychology or to the cultural features and themes of Africa seems totally meaningless to me and, in any event, can be of little practical use because of its blindness. If madness is above all an existential drama or "problem" lived out by the sufferer and the surrounding

---

[14]I have always been deeply convinced of the fundamental dubiousness of descriptive nosography that lacks the support of an explicit nosology and psychopathology to make it clear and consistent.

community, then it is desirable, and indeed indispensable if we are to shed some light on psychiatric methods, to understand the anthropological position of madness in the cultural milieu we are dealing with by first delineating as precisely as possible the elements of the person/personality, thus being better equipped to explain the mechanisms of psychopathological behavior proper.

In other words, the so-called classical, purely descriptive categories are extraneous because they are too general. That they are superficial and artificial and consequently are incapable of giving an adequate account of the psychological, social, human, and clinical realities encountered in Africa is the first thing discovered in the field of practical work when trying to elucidate one's own medical activity. And clear and reasoned "prudence" seems to me to define the very essence of psychiatric intervention.

Beneath the immediately apparent clinical signs is an underlying structure of latent elements that give rise to those signs and shed light on them. Gaining a thorough understanding of these latent elements (which form the point of departure for the organization and disorganization of the systems of the personality) is, in my opinion, essential to the work of a clinician who cares about bringing intelligence and logic to his practice. The formulation and systematization of an adequate nosology (as the groundwork for intelligibility) must be rooted in these latent elements of African anthropology.

In an even more general way, I maintain that any truly scientific nosology should be able to fit in and relate coherently to a more global and more systematic view: that of the corresponding theory of personality, which is itself none other than the formalized expression of the specific anthropological projection of the cultural frame of reference.

In short, apart from (or beyond) academic disputes of a supposedly methodological nature, any rational systems of psychology and psychopathology should be able to break out of the false factual "naïveté" (clinical, experimental, fundamental, etc.) in which these disciplines have become entrenched and should clearly state from the outset the anthropological principles on which their theory of personality is based, thus giving consistency to their findings (with the knowledge that any anthropological doctrine, even one with universal pretensions, is, in the last analysis, merely one point of view among many).

CHAPTER TWO

The Position and Functions
of the Therapist in the
Traditional African Universe

Within the restricted framework of this chapter, I could not, nor would I attempt to, make a painstaking and exhaustive examination of all the ways of training traditional therapists and all the methods used in their practices. Rather I should like to put forward, quite simply, certain information relevant to the present analysis.

For a more detailed and technical account of the various programs for training practitioners, of their

sociocultural status, as well as of the principal diagnostic and therapeutic procedures they use, I refer the
reader to the works already mentioned along with
others that will be cited in the course of this chapter (in
particular, Adler and Zempleni, 1972; Beattie, 1964;
Bourguignon, 1968; Evans-Pritchard, 1937; Jaulin,
1966; Maupoil, 1961; Monfouga-Nicolas, 1972; and
Rouch, 1960).

I shall purposely focus closely on diagnostic procedures based on divination. Thus my analysis will
fall — intentionally — within the anthropological framework of diagnostic interpretation involving mantic
practices, rather than within that of "physical" divination involving anatomy and physiology. What interests
us for our present purpose is the structure of diagnostic
divination in relation to the mentality of people seeking
consultation. In this regard, divination, like all interpretive systems, rests on a whole universe of representations. At the same time, however, it also constitutes a
specific mode of knowledge, with its objects, rules, and
laws. There is a logic to the operations performed and a
coherent classification in terms of a way of thinking.
Lastly — and what interests us especially — mantic interpretation brings order to a whole series of meanings,
with respect to one another and in relation to a
principle-signifier, itself linked to the cultural
significate. The same is probably true of all interpretation; in this case, the chain made up of sign, signifier,
and signified appears more clearly in terms of its various
interconnections.

We shall also see that divination, as a system of
thought, seeks to bring coherence and order even to

the laws of nature, thereby doing away with what is called chance. To summarize, the whole system, along with the divination procedures as actually performed, is based on, and underwritten by, the one true word: of God or the Ancestor, as the case may be, through the intermediary of a genie or spirit. The real vehicle of the mantic process, which gives it structure, meaning, and, in the end, the stamp of validity, is the genie, the personification of natural law.

In Black Africa we find two major types of divination:

1. *Inspired divination*, including all the techniques of so-called possession, is aimed ultimately at plumbing the deeper psychic layers of professional adepts, adepts in states of trance, induced and directed by a master. The best known example of such possession is that of the Bori cult among the Hausa, but this method of interrogation is used throughout Africa.

2. *Deductive divination* is "objective," employing a material vehicle, and the diviner's task consists more narrowly, in terms of operations and interpretations, of examining the evidence (series of mantic configurations) and drawing conclusions therefrom, adhering rigorously to the internal logic and laws of the science of divination.

But why should we take such an interest in these practices? Quite simply because, in the realm of the traditional African diagnostician's operations and procedures, divination is an important, though not exclusive, facet of his profession. So if we hope to understand the meaning of concepts concerning sickness, mental derangement, etc., it seems essential that we try to grasp, at least in terms of their basic principles, not only the concrete operational modalities of divination but also the conceptual associations of such practices within the coherent universe of thought to which they belong.

At base, the psychiatrist, the same as the diviner, demonstrates his competence when, faced with an unusual constellation of symptoms, he succeeds not only in fitting the concrete case as a whole into the repertoire of recognized knowledge but also in providing a satisfactory interpretation against a background, necessarily, of an anthropological system of belief, which in turn comprehends a theory (or prototheory) of the person/personality and its vicissitudes.

I should like to point out that, in Black Africa, traditional practitioners enjoy a solid standing in society. It is estimated that about 90 % of the population continues to seek their services, along with — or independently from — those of modern medicine. A doctor working in a modern hospital center or dispensary soon learns from everyday experience that the large majority of his patients, even while he is treating them, continues to receive, at the same time, treatment by traditional methods. At the level of daily practice, it seems clear and obvious that traditional medicine still meets certain needs, or at least wishes, of patients and their families. Indeed, that is a well-known and uncontestable fact.

Moreover, here and there, to a greater or lesser degree, present-day governments as well as certain African universities have made realistic efforts over the last decade to use traditional medical knowledge. We know, too, that numerous research groups have been established — in botany, pharmacology, medical therapy — and are already in operation. In a number of countries, we are witnessing a rapprochement between the modern hospital and traditional practitioners, notably in pediatrics and general medicine (i.e., at the National University of Cameroon in Yaounde), but also in psychiatry. Understandably, it was in the latter branch of medicine that the first overtures were made; indeed, in that field, more conspicuously than in others, progress has been made in understanding and exploring traditional African techniques. Among the pioneers in this area was Father Lambo, the Nigerian founder of the first therapeutic villages to be integrated into the community in conformity with the African way of life and thought. A few years later, the staff of the University of Dakar-Fann (Senegal), under the leadership of Father Collomb, helped bring attention to the usefulness and efficacy, in the traditional world, of indigenous African methods for the care and treatment of patients suffering from mental disorders.

This trend, showing an openness and a desire to understand, is — it must be emphasized — rather recent. Actually, it coincides historically with the period in which African countries gained national independence. This new desire and new direction also express the need for authenticity, applying the ideology of some of the African intelligentsia and certain political groups to a specific sector. It is in such terms that the idea was expressed as early as 1961 by one of its most brilliant proponents, Cheikh Hamidou Kane (1961), in his celebrated book, *Ambiguous Adventure:*

We have an innate sense of medicine. Imported
diseases have ravaged us. Today we are dying of
poverty for, without money, the doctor rarely
gives good care. Yet not long ago, we got along very
well . . . . Must a list be made of our medical
powers? . . . We treat the chronic cough that goes
by the name of tuberculosis. Only by accident did
anyone ever die of it . . . . It was not so virulent as
the imported tuberculosis that is currently deci-
mating us. We used to cure leprosy, insanity,
epilepsy; fractures, no matter how serious, did not
last a week. We had remedies against illnesses for
which the cure has not yet been found. Were we
capable of nothing, then, as we are made to feel
every day?

The health of individuals is one of the major concerns
of traditional African society. The great cohesiveness
implicit in daily community life in Black Africa very
definitely explains the important role played by the
various traditional practitioners and doctors within the
group.

Illness is not a negligible source of disorder, and very
early, in an effort to ensure well-being, peace, and security, people developed numerous institutions with a
preventive or curative function, protecting both the individual (in his psychoorganic entirety) and the group
(or sociocultural whole) against various forms of
assault.

The external is aggressive. If man does not conquer
it, it destroys man, and makes him a victim of
tragedy. A sore which is neglected does not heal,

but becomes infected to the point of gangrene. A child who is not educated goes backward. A society which is not governed destroys itself [Kane, 1961, p. 79].

Practitioners serve as indispensable mediators, detecting the causes of aggression and reducing the violence that erupts from the conflicts that develop within the human microcosm (man opposing man) [whence the hierarchical multiplicity of institutions for arbitrating potential conflicts, to such an extent that all possible types of cases have, theoretically, been foreseen] or that arise from the disquieting realm of the surrounding mesocosm with its implacable laws (the "natural" world), preserving or reestablishing physical or mental well-being as well as general concord within the group. Agents of consensus, guarantors of the culture, practitioners hold the principles of harmony and equilibrium, which all people need.

According to Lambo (1961), "in African culture reality lies in the realm of the soul and not in that of internal or external things. . . . Reality lies, not in the relationship between man and things, but in that of men with the spirits."

The practitioner's social position has from time immemorial been an honored and esteemed one. In Nigeria, for instance, the diagnostician *(atai idong)* and the traditional doctor *(diong ibok)* used to be at the top of the social ladder; united in a powerful secret society, they practiced their art bedecked in attire symbolizing their attributes (a great tunic and a headdress of plaited vines). The role of the official practitioners is underscored in all the narratives relating the history of the great African kingdoms; both types were respected not only for their diagnostic and healing powers but also, and above all, for their ability to communicate with the spirit doubles, to analyze a situation in its entirety with a perfect understanding of the circumstances and the milieu, and, lastly, to divine the favorable or unfavorable outcome of a decision concerning a personal undertaking or a political or military action. The most renowned among them play the role of "royal adviser" and serve as modern technocrats.

Among the activities of a traditional practitioner, the manipulation and interpretation of signifiers is essential. Such procedures dealing with symbols always accompany, sustain, and support the pharmacological action proper.

Moreover we know that in Black Africa, "for the sufferer, the distress that is felt is often only an epiphenomenon. The true cause of sickness is of a moral order" (Huard, cited in Sonolet, 1971, p. 19).[1]

Organic disease is not denied, not at all. However, and this seems fundamental here, beneath the manifest syndromic array, a latent dimension always lies hidden. In short, to the traditional way of thinking, the ap-

[1]"African concepts of disease... are much more oriented toward what one calls 'man as a whole,' that is, man within his natural environment, in his society, his group, his family, at work or at rest. To the African mind, everything is bound up together, and any difficult situation, whether it be personal, social, or due to the environment, can be ameliorated through use of the appropriate 'medicine,' directed either against a person's enemies or against the evil spirits that are often blamed for people's ills. In its fundamental outline, this mental approach is not limited to the thinking of Africa; psychiatrists can find very similar examples in the mental attitudes of Western peoples" (Poynter, 1971, p. 6).

parent, immediate, mechanistic cause explains nothing. As a matter of fact, that cause can be no more than coincidental; the truly efficient cause is the result of conflicting dynamic forces that are hidden, or at any rate are not immediately apparent or accessible. It follows that the African conception of medicine and disease is a dynamic one. The role of the practitioner is always that of someone whose task it is to bring to light (and lay bare) the fundamental conflict that has caused the patient to be personally afflicted with one disorder or another under certain specific circumstances.

Thus medical "action" is always both offensive and defensive. In certain figures of speech, its ties can be discerned with the basic activities of practical life: waging war, hunting and fishing, as well as farming. This explains the fact that within the professional category of practitioners there is a division of labor between the sexes along symbolic lines. To be more specific, in highly simplified outline, a man apprehends the meaning of signs, projects himself into the past, the present, or the future, and prevents or checks sickness; a woman, as procreator and provider of life, "mothers" and gives new life to the patient during possession.[2]

In either case, whatever the practitioner's orientation or method of working, professional status can be acquired only by completing a course of training. This

[2]In the anthropological perspective of traditional Black Africa, woman is a prime mover and vital element essential to the good functioning and continuation of social institutions. The source and seat of fertility and prosperity, she is also the guarantor of custom. She preserves the traditional methods of healing; in particular, her role in the techniques of trance and possession, though not exclusive, has often — and for good reason — been considered preeminent.

initiation, as it is called, may be gone through individually or in a group, under the direction of an elder (an initiated master practitioner), who is also responsible for the oral transmission of a body of organized knowledge. Initiation consists mainly of the novices' acquisition of symbols, a semantic tradition, and a code, along with their active practical or "technical" training, as it were, in touch with reality. The duration and degree of complexity of the initiation vary with the type of activity the postulant intends to pursue. There are, of course, a hierarchy of training regimens and functions in connection with a rank order, and a hierarchy based on individual competence and experience, which combine to enhance or diminish a practitioner's reputation. All these variables oblige us to analyze each situation separately:

•that of the practitioner responsible for diagnosis in a broad sense (that is, for the detection and interpretation of "signs");

•that of the practitioner proper (generalist or specialist) acting individually to cure and/or prevent disease;

•that of professional groups in charge of the therapeutic techniques of possession (male, female, or mixed groups of therapists).

Although divination is known and has been practiced in all human societies (see Caquot and Leibovici, 1968), African societies unquestionably figure among those that have consolidated it to the greatest extent. The mantic tradition stands out very clearly in Africa, not only as an ordered and coherent set of symbolic operations but also as a mental system that is intellectually rational and socially legitimate, as attested to in the ever-increasing number of scholarly works devoted to this subject.

In Black Africa, far from being a marginal "magical" or aberrant phenomenon, divination is a regular, normal procedure that a group or individual turns to when important decisions must be made concerning public or private life; it fits coherently into the overall web of social thinking (cf. Labouret, 1922; Monteil, 1931). The mantic act takes a rational form, with stages and a logical structure that can be laid out and formalized. Entering into the fields of law, government, politics, and medicine, divination and its procedures would seem to constitute:

> . . . an official agency of legitimation, which, in the event of choices fraught with consequences for the equilibrium of communities, offers socially "objective" decisions, that is, independent of the wishes of the parties in question and benefiting from a general consensus on the part of the social body, which places this type of response above dispute [Vernant, 1974, p. 10].

In this sense, divination practiced by eminent and recognized specialists, analyzing and interpreting an important social situation for a "prince," for example, differs in no way, in terms of the substance and nature of the diviner's role, from the activity of highly placed technocrats, manipulating mathematical models on the basis of data and weighing risks (intermediate or long-term) to make their forecasts and offer advice. In either case, it is clearly understood that the final decision rests with the prince or the political authority. It should be pointed out that divination assumes many forms, and it may be useful to review them briefly here.

Interpreting signs and events in the fate of a private petitioner, divination arrives at conclusions by considering elements that take into account the past and the present as well as the future.[3]

> It is important, then, especially at difficult times (involving death, disease, witchcraft, misfortune, rites of passage) or when a major decision is called for, to see things more clearly, to lay bare what is hidden, to apprehend what is possible and to adapt thereto and make a wise choice [Thomas and Luneau, 1975, p. 160].

Directed toward the unknown and uncontrolled, looked on as a way of finding out what is hidden or strange, "objective" divination, in the strict sense, is essentially rational in that it is an effort of the human mind to decipher a message, bringing into play a series of deductive and interpretive techniques based on the use of chance sequences. But besides these "objective" deductive techniques centered on the manipulation of paraphernalia and the interpretation of object configurations in strict conformity with rules and a code, techniques involving inspiration must be mentioned, reminiscent of the frenzied divination or "inspired mad-

---

[3]In Africa, however, unless a prediction in terms of a favorable/unfavorable outcome is at stake, the "future" or what will come to pass is of less concern than the explanation of the troubles disrupting day-to-day life in the present; in any case, the future is thought of only in conjunction with what is and what has been.

ness" described by Plato (communication of knowledge beyond the senses, revelation through ecstacy, poetic visions, dreams).[4] In inspired (or intuitive) divination, the diagnostic procedure may seem more passive. Actually, it requires a special mental state, functioning as an "instrument" that reveals, through ecstacy or trance, a message in a "pathetic" register.[5] Some writers (e.g., Evans-Pritchard, 1937; Paulme, 1956) maintain that there is a certainly similarity between this type of diagnostic practice and that of the ancient Greeks,

[4]Zahan (1970) distinguishes two great modes of divination: "One of these would be based on the apprehension of the relationship between things (intellectual process), while the other, lacking intellectual participation on the part of the diviner, would be based instead on his instrumental role in the divinatory operation (mediumistic process). The diviners who practice the first kind of divination are interpreters; they judge and appreciate the conjunction of the signifiers and the signifieds in a divinatory theme. Those devoted to the second augural mode are the 'messengers'; practically speaking, they do not 'touch' the content of the communication. The former establish the oracle, the latter reveal it.

"The interpreter-diviners employ divinatory equipment, objects which permit them to exercise their intuition and clairvoyance and with whose aid they establish the augural theme according to the needs of their clients. . . .

"The messenger-diviners use little or no divinatory material. . . . The augural objects are replaced by the very person of the diviner. . . . He enters into a trance and personally makes the voyage to the Souls, from whence he reports the messages awaited by the clients.

"The distinction drawn between the two types of diviners and, consequently, between the two great African divinatory modes, should not make us lose sight of the single psychological presupposition which underlies all these practices, that is, the conception of the constitution of the human person" (the existence of the double, its mobility in comparison with the soul, the continuity between the living and the dead)" (pp. 86–87).

[5]The distinction lies, it seems to me, in the fact that a "pathetic" message cannot be transmitted directly by the practitioner himself; he uses skilled professional "messengers," who have been trained to receive messages, while he, the diagnostician, remains perfectly lucid. Thus there are adepts at entering a state of trance, specialists whose role is to be questioned, under precise technical conditions orchestrated by a master diviner.

namely, the oracles, in particular the Pythia of Delphi.

It is true that the Nzakara of Chad often seek the cause of disease or death in their dreams (Retel-Laurentin, 1969, p. 9), for the "spirits" are thought to express their grievances and wishes when hypnotic dissociation brings on the dreams of humans. And yet are the meaning of messages in dreams and, in a more general way, the motives and ends concerning spirits but also the personality identical throughout the world? Do anthropological perspectives everywhere merge into one? The *ba do nganga,* for example, identify "evildoers" while leaping wildly during dances of possession. In the Cameroon, certain female practitioners are the divinatory vehicles of the *facalao* genies that possess them, whereas the male practitioners are sought out by the *mbilda* genie. The Ndembu practitioners of Zambia enter into direct contact with "powers" that speak through the diviner's mouth (Turner, 1968). And so on.

But deductive divination (either "objective" or rational) is practiced far more frequently and will claim more of our attention, for it is a form of diagnostic or prophylactic counsel that anyone can seek at will. Aimed at establishing a diagnosis or prognosis when a decision looms or illness strikes, this type of active divination interprets real events by analyzing the configurations of objects arranged by aleatory procedures or by reading ideographic or pictographic signs; it seeks to "decipher the universe as if it were a question of a text in which one would find the order of the world inscribed, a tablet on which the gods would have traced out men's destinies" (Vernant, 1974, p. 24).

Actually, it is a question of attempting to interpret chance in order to give it *meaning* and *structure*. It follows that just as there is a certain order in the arrangement of elements that make up the human microcosm, giving rise to a symbolic interpretive reading, so does deductive divination systematically seek homology and correspondence in terms of some code. There is a meaningful relationship between the configurations obtained through chance procedures at the time of consultation—like so many arrangements, dispositions, and combinations, which reflect, on a small scale, not only the human microcosm but also the invisible mesocosm (the seat of the "natural" laws of chance) and, ultimately, the whole cosmic order (or law).

> Divination focuses on sequences of certain events, about which one seeks counsel precisely because they are of a haphazard order; through its procedures it applies a general logic to them, which leads to the exclusion of chance in the web of events, to the elimination of the random in interpreting relations of temporal succession, with the margin of unpredictability inherent therein, on the model of structural relationships of homology and correspondence, which are inscribed and traceable in a segment of space [Vernant, 1974, p. 17].

Consequently, and very briefly, it can be said that all observable phenomena, relating to terrestrial or celestial elements, animal or human, physiological or psychological, animate or inanimate, can serve as signs, which accounts for the multiplicity of techniques and the diversity of tools:[6]

•the use of such natural signs as the heavenly bodies — the sun and the moon, the planets, stars and constellations — rain, storms, etc.;

•the use of the earth, of soil, sand, stones, and shells (cowries), of patterns and markings on the ground (geomancy);

•the use of vegetable matter, such as seeds, nuts, branches, fruit, and lamellae of plants *(kindani-sin-zu,* for example, among the Mundang);

•the use of animals, including observation of the behavior of wild animals (e.g., the jackal among the Dogon, the trap-door spider among the Nzakara[7]),

---

[6]Different practices may also, in some cases, be related to the culture forming the frame of reference (e.g., hunting, pastoralist, fishing, or farming societies).

[7]Gaspard and Françoise Towo-Atangana have transcribed some of the *mvet* tales of the Cameroon (the *mvet* being a musical instrument the traditional poets use to accompany their tales). One of them, *"Nged-nso-fa,"* tells of using the trap-door spider for divination:

> You have fallen ill in the chest,
> You are sick in the morning, you are sick in the evening,
> Aching in the head, aching in the body;
> Your members grow weak,
> Your eyes become yellow,
> Your legs are pale and covered with scales.
> And now you come to consult the oracles.
> You have something in this village,
> If it is not taken away.
> You are dying and leaving your wealth.
> You have three sons here;
> Let one go before,
> Let one go behind;
> Your middle son,
> The one who follows the eldest,
> Speech lies hidden in his belly

the examination of entrails (necromancy), and divination using fowl (gallinomancy);

•the use of such objects as knucklebones, dice (the Thonga of Zambia and Malawi), sticks (the Venda of Rhodesia), beads (the Agni of Ivory Coast), or calabash fragments *(kindani-a-piri* among the Mundang);

•the use of the human body, with reference to facial features, to physical aspects of the newborn, etc.

The answer that emerges after questioning by the simple procedures used by private individuals themselves, rather than through the intermediary of specialists, follows the logic of alternatives (a diagnosis based on a more or less long chain of yes or no responses). Thus the opposition of thesis and antithesis often tends to reduce this approach to a step-by-step application for a probabilist process to the elements (which do not vary much) of the divination code.[8]

To give some idea of what is involved, it should be pointed out that certain mantic procedures require great skill on the part of the practitioner. For example, according to Adler and Zempleni (1972), in an averge seance a Mundang diviner responds some 200 times to the casting of lots,[9] with each manipulation requiring a

---

If he does not give voice to it.
You are dying and leaving your riches there, in truth.
If it is not as I say,
May the trap-door spider carry me off to the grave,
    among the dead.
[G. Towo-Atangana, 1967, pp. 337–339.]

[8]One can therefore contrast, as Park (1963) has done, "mechanical" or analytical divination with "emotive" divination (which is actually drama).

[9]It should be noted that an experienced diagnostician with a reputation for his divinatory abilities will know how to interpret all possible configurations, which are paired very precisely with codified interpretations.

score of gestures to separate the stones by pairs, or about 50,000 gestures per session. Other methods, such as geomancy (cf. Hébert, 1961), have a much more supple syntax, which makes for a remarkable economy of gestures and time (with the systems for classifying figures being consequently reduced to mnemonic techniques).[10]

Formal analysis of geomantic procedures shows that the diviner's interpretation sometimes involves a highly complex intellectual process, calling on logical reasoning structured on mathematical lines (arithmetical or algebraic). We have come a long way from the simplistic prejudices of the nineteenth century, which saw in these practices only magic and/or ignorance. The fact is, though, it is still too easy to talk about what we know nothing of, taking comfort in our own ignorance.

In the words of Jaulin (1966), "it all unfolds as if the structure of the divinatory system were not simply an abstract construct of thought that facilitates one's understanding of reality, but as if the structures of the two — of the system and of reality — were one and the same, concrete and precise" (p. 179). As a matter of fact, the essential thing is not so much to discover a solution as to find a way of contemplating factors believed to be vectors of reality.

It is hard to imagine what that implies in terms of intellectual labor and memory capacity.

[10]The Mundang practitioner bases his interpretations on an algorithm applied throw by throw (each time he must first construct his class of objects and then select the pertinent elements). The geomancer bases his interpretations on a table of preexisting signs (signs represented by one or two graphic elements indicating odd and even, respectively; each sign is defined by a "house," that is, a fixed location on the table, and sometimes by astrological connotations of a zodiacal nature).

Passing from sign to structure requires reflective effort; there is nothing automatic about it, as one might think. Starting from an empirical discipline of pure observation, divination has risen to the rank of a deductive science proper, which can be formalized. It can be described as such within an anthropological framework in which people recognize a correspondence and homology between, on the one hand,

•the elements of the immediate human microcosmos,

•the elements of the mesocosmos (intermediary, invisible), and

•the macrocosmic whole (diverse structures encompassing the whole)

and, on the other hand,

•chance configurations and sequences which, in terms of the law of numbers, appear to be so many elements of a single coherent overall structure.

Or stated otherwise, if the universe is structured and coherent, then the whole complex that makes up the totality of possible chance configurations is structured and coherent as well.

In concrete terms, divination has passed from empiricism (involving *a posteriori* findings with respect to specific isolated cases that are contingent and unpredictable) to deductive *a priori* knowledge, which is systematic, codified, and capable of prediction (within an appropriate anthropological structure that views the universe as a structure) and which bears on abstract, necessary, universal objects:

> It is a veritable science, universal in its object and its way of apprehending it, necessary in its laws, de-

ductive and *a priori* in its procedures, still sus-
tained, of course, by observation of reality and the
concrete, but now seeking the invariable, the
abstract, the general, in short, the rational [Jaulin,
1966].

Proceeding like a scientist, the diviner examines the
facts and draws conclusions therefrom according to an
internal logic, which in no way excludes a concern for
verification; the cross-checks that are conducted,
especially in more serious situations, often make the
diviner's task arduous and complex. Diagnostic and
prognostic procedures consist in long and sometimes
painful trials, as do all "technical" operations aimed at
mastering man's destiny.[11]

Consequently from the perspective of African anthropology (with its panstructured universe), no one
can seriously contest the cosmic connection of the mantic process. Logical (in terms of its operations), scientific
and technical (in terms of its methods and specialized
practitioners), rational deductive divination is, of
course, a profane technical procedure, but the cosmic
dimension, by way of symbolic relations with the structured African universe, is always present.[12] As a practice

[11]The practice of divination and the manipulations it requires can put the
diviner in danger. That is why the Mundang *pa-kindani*, for example,
smears himself with numerous medicines before each seance and takes
drugs to fortify himself in advance against attacks by the "local spirits" that
are stirred up by his intervention. That is to say that the manipulation of
technical and natural forces is often a perilous undertaking.

[12]The messenger-diviner (in his "dramatic," "inspired" role) is closer,
however, to the cosmic dimension than is the interpreter-diviner (the first
practitioner may "die" and "come back to life," having entered the world of
the spirits; the second always remains at the more immediate level of ordinary human beings).

that is highly charged with meaning, divination cannot be an isolated technique, standing alone. It may be accompanied by sacrifices, preceded or followed by prayers or invocations; the diviner may consult God, but he also sounds out the "forces of nature."[13] Since everything is linked in a coherent universe, the diagnosis will always be a diagnosis of synthesis (of totality).

The judicial aspect of divination is equally striking. In comparing and verifying the portents, the practitioner proceeds as if he were examining the documentary evidence in a legal case. In order to answer the questions put to him, that is, to reach a decision regarding the client's situation, he manipulates, sorts, and orders the facts, comparing them with the "Law" and the traditional legal code, and only then does he issue a judgment accordingly.

Today the material and social positions of certain practitioners seem modest, for their skill is always meagerly rewarded. In rural areas they are tillers of the soil like everyone else, though firmly ensconced in the daily life of the local leaders whom they serve as confidants and heeded advisers. In large urban communities, many of them enjoy a very high reputation, evidenced by a lifestyle to match. There, as anyone familiar with Africa knows, they continue to have a real and not negligible political influence, and it is common knowl-

[13]In Dahomey, Fa is considered to be "the spirit or very essence of divination"; at the same time he is a manifestation of Mawu (the divine Word), being the "speech" of Mawu. He is the object of great respect in the eyes of men and also on the part of all the other *vudu* spirits. The *bokono* (diviner), father of the secret and mother of the truth, is the "messenger of Fa" among the Fan and the Yoruba; he is diviner, priest and sacrificer, pharmacist and doctor, all in one (cf. Maupoil, 1961).

edge that they are regularly consulted by government officials (chiefs of state and ministers included). It almost seems as if they were lending their support in a way, bestowing traditional legitimacy on modern political power with all its uncertainties, risks, and anxieties.

Thus the diviner serves as keeper of the codes that make it possible to decipher the various messages addressed to man,[14] to the society in which he lives, and to all that is bound up with man's fate. "He possesses the skill of penetrating the universe of signs, which mediates between the world and the human being, and by ordering it to his own method, he is able to make it clarify the situation at hand" (Zahan, 1970, p. 81). The traditional practitioner clearly plays a prominent role in the cultural life of Africa. He is consulted in connection with any important event in life (a journey, the construction of a house, birth, the naming of a child, circumcision, marriage, illness, death, etc.). When a man is uneasy before the inexplicable, he needs an indication or interpretation of anything that is likely to thwart his plans and hence upset his personal life or that of his village, or even of his country. In seeking such counsel, he is also seeking assurance in the form of sanction to his undertakings. Thus the diviner's task consists not only in answering the question in general terms (favorable/unfavorable) but also, more specifically, in indicating the measures that must be taken (e.g., the sacrifices that must be made) to enhance the auspiciousness of the

[14]"Kings have prescribed destinies just like men, and seers who probe the future know it" (Niane, 1960, p. 41).

situation (if the answer is favorable) or counteract its inauspiciousness (if the answer is unfavorable).

Sickness that does not yield to the usual remedies but takes on an alarming aspect is the most common event prompting individuals to consult the average practitioner. Consequently, he is trained to serve as a medical adviser as well, or in any case he is at least versed in the pharmacological properties of various plants. For example, the Dahomean *bokono* (cf. Maupoil, 1961) knows how to prepare medicines; he administers laxatives and diuretics, applies poultices, practices cupping and bleeding. In addition, he maintains a hospice near his house consisting of one or more large residences where patients stay while under treatment.

When someone is suffering from an organic complaint and consults a traditional practitioner, it is never to confirm or deconfirm the organic diagnosis itself, in the Western sense of the term or according to the Western intellectual approach. Leprosy, yaws, smallpox, dysentery, fracture, or sprain, for instance, will already have been identified by some member of the more or less extended family group, and a form of treatment will always have been begun. Actually, the traditional doctor does not intervene at the onset of illness, or at least not in the majority of cases. When he is consulted, it is very specifically to determine the deeper causes that abnormally prolong and/or aggravate the illness, despite the natural medication that has been successful in similar circumstances.

In reality, a structural diagnosis is asked of the traditional practitioner, which is aimed at determining the meaning of the illness (rather than its immediate cause) in order to relieve existential anxiety in terms of the patient's total experience. In short, the practitioner is expected to seek out the elements of a deeper conflict, knowing that the present extrinsic disorder is, according to traditional thinking, only an incidental cause. The problem will always be to find out how to tie the clinical case in, how to determine its place and classify it within the complex relationships of a universe that is looked on as panstructured.

Therefore, from the outset, the traditional practitioner's activity is on another level than that of the usual Western medical relationship (leaving aside psychological conversation of a dynamic order). In essence, it will consist of bringing to light the unapparent, hidden elements that make up the conflict structure reflected in the clinical case, for mental as well as organic disorders and even, in a general way, for unhappy experiences, including the failures encountered in everyday life. Hence the practitioner's concern is to carry out painstaking investigations at the level of the various fields that make up the total personality itself and determine the quality of its structural organization, both immediate and remote.

The seance develops in three successive stages to arrive at a synthesis establishing the final diagnosis, which, at the same time, always provides an interpretation of the case as a whole:

First stage: the mantic examination proper, consisting of detailed questioning of the different relational poles that form the very foundation of the patient's psychological makeup as person/personality, with interrogation in terms of pairs of opposites—stability (favorable)/

instability (unfavorable); in short, examination of the elements constituting the sociocosmic universe in which the supplicant has his roots, and precisely from which his sickness (affliction) seems to uproot him.

Second stage: determination of a diagnosis through meaning, always followed by formulation of a general prognosis.

Third stage: prescription, that is, indicating the methods of treatment and initiating the therapeutic procedure.

The Mundang diviner (cf. Adler and Zempleni, 1972) practices at the edge of the bush, where, seated on a flat stone under a tree, he works on a "divining floor" on which a figure is traced out with numerous little pebbles, consisting of three arcs oriented toward the south. Each arc gives him information having a positive/negative valence. Through a system of drawing by lots, he examines each element of the three sets that make up the inclusive contexts of the disorder. Thus the *pa-kindani* is confronted with 117 figures aligned on the ground: 43 figures are grouped in seven sections, with each section containing a sequence of information concerning the state of the village community (general outlook, weather, land and space, water, local spirits, categories of persons, the moon, and the rain); 62 figures are grouped in eight sections (reason, spiritual principles associated with the head of the family, food and drink, the state of the wives of the head of the family, the physical state of the patient's child, the state of the therapist, the state of the assistant therapists); and 12 figures represent the *sin-ri* that cause the illness (affliction), that is, the rupture of bonds (through conflict).

Once again, the traditional practitioner does not, in the main, work from the usual external clinical categories, which are visible, well defined, and known to all. His role is to establish a satisfactory connection between the illness already there — resistant, recognized, and manifest — with the latent universe of meanings. His goal, in fact, is a general interpretation of the ailment.

Considering again the Mundang divining floor and, more specifically, the three arcs:

1. the outer arc provides information about the village community (the context in which the illness appears);

2. the center arc provides information about the places, things, and persons that the patient will be interacting with during the therapeutic sessions;

3. the inner arc provides information about the agents of "possession": village group, family, therapist.

I should also like to point out here, without going into detail (which can be found in the study of Adler and Zempleni, 1972), that the diagnostic procedure is based on a system of proceeding from genus to species, from the general to the particular, from the outside to the inside. There are relationships of inclusion between the semantic fields that are successively explored by the diviner, which makes his praxis similar to the Western technique of (well-conducted) differential diagnosis.

But the method itself is always synthetic, because the totality of a complex situation must be accounted for with all its tortuous interrelationships. From the perspective of African anthropology, nothing important can be revealed through a process of analytical isolation, for in fact everything is connected and in motion.[15]

During a divining session, therefore, the traditional practitioner gives the impression of leaving little room for the expression of the patient's feelings and symptoms, as he concentrates on reading the signs immediately apparent on the divining floor. Actually, knowing the state of the overall relations within the community, as well as the temperaments, habits, and problems of its individual members, he is working on two "texts" at once: he adapts the facts of the real-life situation to the mantic information, as Adler and Zempleni (1972) have pointed out. The divining act proper, however, leaves no place for the direct expression of the patient's separate emotions and symptoms. Only at the stage of the structural diagnosis (the second stage) does the practitioner achieve a synthesis between "objective" and "subjective" elements, knowing that in

[15]African thought processes are always based on a frame of reference and point of view that are synthetic and dynamic, because thinking, itself — a point I shall repeatedly stress — is integrated, as a modality, into a panstructured universe, that is, a universe where everything has a place, has sense and meaning within a coherent whole.

The analytical point of view (breaking the universe down into so many distinct elements), with its technological bent, supports and fosters, in my opinion, thinking that is ultimately stripped of signifiers, in a world that is similarly stripped and a universe that is no longer a universe.

It is no doubt always tempting to break down beings and things in order to get a better technical grasp of them. Yet at the same time that one breaks down, dissects, and analyzes, by that very act one loses existence and, *a fortiori*, sense and meaning.

As the founder of modern analytical thought, Descartes can be credited with leaving a threefold legacy, variously appraised, consisting of three facets of a single problem; (a) the dualism that gave rise to mechanism but also, one tends to forget, to the idea of natural man (human nature) — the most enduring archaism of Western thinking; (b) the leveling of the human universe; and (c) the development of the pure technological object.

any event his diagnosis must meet with the approval of the client and his family. Agreement is necessary since it is inevitably a question of interpretation.

When the diviner's interpretation of the case is accepted, it can then be said that the *pa-kindani*'s word is absolute; but the *pa-kindani* himself constitutes precisely the symbolic field of the community. Moreover, the prescriptions, which are also addressed to the client, never concern him alone, "the present and future state of the client being closely bound up with the lucky or unlucky arrangement of each of the elements that mark out and form the collective symbolic field within which his illness develops" (Adler and Zempleni, 1972, p. 88).

Therefore, far from being pure speculation — intellectual, magical, or gratuitous — deductive divination is a social and psychological tool of the first order, an effective instrument of control, an official agency of legitimation, which helps considerably to eliminate sources of uncontrolled conflict in social relations. Consulting a diviner is an essential step in the social process of readjustment that is necessary in certain crises that threaten the equilibrium of the group (cf. Lévi-Strauss, 1958; Park, 1963; Turner, 1968).

Although treatment may require close supervision of the actions the client is supposed to carry out (for it is necessary to ensure the efficacy of the individual in the real world as defined by social classifications), divination is not, nor can it be, a means of influence. As Adler and Zempleni (1972) aptly note, "the position of the petitioner, whether a private client or the community, is more like that of a user of some service" (p. 209), a service that is performed by a sophisticated machine, by a technician whose competence extends to the whole of the sociocultural field as defined by the categories examined. It is possible, moreover, to consult as many practitioners as one wishes and then to compare, on one's own, the various diagnoses put forward. Thus we perceive the social importance of traditional practitioners.

We can see, then, that the work of a diviner requires high intellectual capacities (the ability to understand and transmit messages, technical skill in reading and deciphering configurations, the ability to synthesize, and a thorough understanding of the culture) combined with perceptive insight into the delicate problems of human relations; to practice divination it is not enough, as one might think, to have a "gift" or to be supposedly under the influence of some supernatural power. Furthermore, learning the technique of the various procedures often requires 12 to 15 years of training before the most intelligent and quick-witted students are able to interpret the signs and configurations correctly, and even then only after several years of supervision. As Zahan (1970) remarks:

> The function of diviner does not tolerate improvisation; on the contrary, to become a "seer" it is indispensable to follow a long and hard apprenticeship. It is often even necessary to undergo a veritable initiation, a transformation similar to those which lead man to the sources of religious life, to God [p. 82].

Whether the aptitude to become a diviner is transmitted through heredity, whether it emerges out of some special experience, or whether it is acquired during a long, difficult, and costly apprenticeship, the practice of divination nevertheless requires exhaustive training under the direction and supervision of an experienced master. This training tends to be comprehensive rather than technical in the narrow sense, a broad course, more a spiritual undertaking in the case of training for inspired divination (in regard to Azande diviners see Evans-Pritchard, 1937, and for the Baluba see Tiarko Fourche and Morlighem, 1939). And quite strikingly, it is the same when it is a case of training perception, memory, and judgment in the apprenticeship to acquire the working skills for deductive divination (in regard to the Bantu of southeast Africa, see Junod, 1912, vol. 2, pp. 564–568).

The training (i.e., initiation) of the *bokono* among the Fon and Yoruba of Dahomey (see Maupoil, 1961) is typical in that it mobilizes the whole of the psychic system, conscious and unconscious, and that it prepares the postulant for the exercise of diagnostic, prognostic, and therapeutic functions, bearing on all fields of human activity.

Among the *vudu*,[16] Fa is unquestionably the most

[16]It should be noted that in Dahomey the term *vudu* tends to be used to designate everything of a spiritual order (terrestrial and celestial forces, protective genies, etc.): "The *vudu* give satisfaction to mortals who pray to them individually or collectively; certain *vudu* have the special ability to reveal the future; the faithful come to consult them...*vudu* may possess someone serving them, mounting that person's head" (Maupoil, 1961, pp. 59–61). The *vudu-no* are the official guardians (formerly subject to the priests of the royal cults). A diviner may honor a number of *vudu*, but he is the priest only of Fa (though Fa is considered to be "master of the *vudu*"), and no one, as a matter of fact, is ever possessed by Fa, who is the bearer and medium of the Word of Mawu.

revered and powerful. Considered the medium (or vector) of the divine Word, Fa is both a general entity (the aggregate of the signs, which no one can know in their entirety) and an individualized principle, so that attached to each human being is a personal Fa, the object of private worship.

In brief outline, the traditional education of a Fon or Yoruba child involves progressive familiarization with Fa, in three stages:

1. *Fa-kwi-we* (at about three to four or five years of age): a servant of Fa (a master diviner) prepares two palm nuts, asks that the child may have a long life, and after stringing the nuts, gives them to the child's parents.

2. *Fa-si-se* (adolescence): "known to Fa," the adolescent receives, as they say, one or two "hands" (nuts in two calabashes).

3. *Fa-ti-te* (maturity): admittance is granted to the sacred grove *(Fazū)* and Fa's sanctuary.

The third stage, bringing fullness of the personality, offers a limited number of postulants the opportunity to become a *bokono*. If an initiate wishes to do so, he becomes the disciple of a devotee of Fa (a master), offering a kid in sacrifice to his master and Fa. He must then go through a long apprenticeship lasting from three to seven years (during which he learns to decipher the various geomantic figures) in order to become a practitioner and a servant of Fa in turn.

There is no "school" (in the usual Western sense of the term), nor do the *bokono*, though they are "servants of Fa," form a sacerdotal body strictly speaking. Normally, to "learn Fa" the postulant must first of all be motivated; then he must join the practice of a Fa diviner. The apprentice assists at seances — listening, observing, and training his attention. To begin with, he learns the 16 basic signs, then the numerous auxiliary signs that guide his master as practitioner; learning the principal signs (names and figurations) takes about two months, whereas learning the secondary signs may require four years. The novice listens closely to the interpretations of the figures that the master offers the clients; he learns to use the paraphernalia and tools of divination (beads, nuts, boards, bones, cowry shells, kola nuts, etc.). In addition, he learns to make amulets and concoct medicines that cure stomach ailments, headaches, eye troubles, sores, fevers, and so on — in short, all the clinical cases that present themselves for treatment in day-to-day practice.

Following a pattern very similar to psychoanalytic training, the neophyte begins with practice sessions under supervision (these take place at dusk, in a courtyard or a hut, and may last from a few minutes to a few hours). Once he is recognized as competent to practice independently, he is solemnly invested in the sacred grove.[17]

Actually, the apprenticeship for Fa divination is considered a course of study without end (Fa is boundless); thus the calling of diviner entails ceaseless perfection. Technical competence, of course, may differentiate one practitioner from another. All, however, enjoy a high

---

[17]The profession of *bokono* is almost exclusively a male preserve. In rare cases it may be practiced by a woman whose intelligence and "virile" character are suited for the service of Fa.

reputation.[18] At the same time confidants, traditional "jurists," counselors, doctors of both body and soul, they serve as mediators and conciliators. They must be honest, sober, and well balanced; they must never lie or take sides in conflicts between individuals or groups.

The *bokono* (the traditional practitioner of Benin) is consulted during pregnancy, at birth, on the occasion of the first menstrual period, before betrothal and marriage, after death, and indeed before any important undertaking. He knows how to sift through things, how to get to the bottom of them; he knows the premonitory value of dreams; he "predicts life and death."[19]

His public role is "to be available to people who are driven to him by the anxieties or vicissitudes of life," to answer their questions, and to help them, to the best of his ability, to regain their equilibrium: "he must tell the whole truth to his clients, pray for them, lead into the sacred wood those for whom the time has come to receive the revelation of their Fa, make the necessary sacrifices. . . . It is he whose intervention is sought, even by servants of the *vudu*, to conjure away physical or mental ills" (Maupoil, 1961, p. 115). His private role is to attend to the worship of his personal Fa and serve as counselor for his family, as well as to gather leaves hav-

[18]And many privileges as well. Under the old kingdoms they were protected from administrative interference, wore special clothing, as mentioned earlier, and shaved their bodies and heads as a mark of distinction.

[19]When the normal exercise of reason yields no solution, he sometimes exploits any special faculties he may possess (e.g., telepathy). In this regard, the indisputable abilities of the great diviner Gedegbe, special adviser to Glebe, King of Dahomey, are exemplary and celebrated. The reader is referred to Maupoil (1961), who knew Gedegbe personally when he was a colonial administrator. As his collaborators, a *bokono* has *kpamega*, who have a knowledge of grasses and leaves.

ing curative properties, which heal when they are con-
sumed, touched, or incorporated into talismans.[20]

If the practitioner must be respected (no one may in-
sult him or lift a hand against him when he is officiating,
on pain of severe punishment), the practitioner for his
part must respect certain precepts, must not violate certain taboos: "He must neither kill nor do harm, neither
steal nor take the wife of another; he should act as a
father and a benefactor." The traditional practitioner's
goodness and the rectitude of his life are highly regarded
qualities, which in any event distingish him from the
"sorcerer" (with whom he is easily confused by
foreigners). The *bokono* "roots out evil, checks it, or
holds it off; he seeks coolness, equilibrium, well-being;
[his task is to] preserve people and the community, not
to kill, to see people killed, or to have them killed"
(Maupoil, 1961, p. 156).

The function of the diviner and that of the healer
(when they are distinct) are necessarily complementary, and the two practitioners play equally important
roles in African societies[21] (whence the frequent confusion of the positions.

---

[20]The practitioner regularly makes sacrifices to ensure the support of his
Fa (at the time of the new moon in particular); he may petition Fa every
week or once a month.

[21]The diviner needs the healer and vice versa. The results of divination
are worthless if they have no effect, so the patient is referred to the doctor.
On the other hand, to ensure conformity, therapeutic actions must be subject to scrupulous supervision by the diviner: "The healers, possessing a
precise but narrow empirical knowledge. . . are assistants in a practice in
which the prescription — in the medical sense, as it were — has been produced by the divinatory process. The religious or pharmacological knowledge that enables them to provide the services expected of them is a closed
form of knowledge. Divided up, partitioned off according to specialty, it is

The social role of the traditional doctor is that of any authority responsible for defending the community. Not content with detecting the active agents of a conflict situation, the cause of existential disorder, he communicates with them, mastering them or using them in a positive sense, consistent with the requirements of equilibrium dictated by community life.

In Zaïre, for example, the *nganga* intervenes with the *simbi* (spirits), with a power to control and direct them, and the Kongo look on him as the great peacemaker and guardian of the community (cf. Buakasa, 1971). His interventions and actions, although mostly concerned with individual troubles, are regarded as barometers of public health. His knowledge is imbued with good sense and conforms to the logic of a way of thinking that serves the community.

Like the West African griot, the traditional healer of central Africa generally has a wide knowledge of the history of lineages; the origin of villages; the relations among clans; the psychology of each member of the community (relatives, neighbors, friends, in-laws); past, present, and potential conflicts; and so on. He relies on this knowledge to maintain or restore, in all circumstances, the necessary equilibrium in relations between the constituent poles that define individual and group life within the community:

•current cultural signifiers (the field of enemies and social competitors);

---

not questioned except as required by the word of the *kindani,* who confers on it its legitimacy" (Adler and Zempleni, 1972, p. 210).

•biolineal existence (the field of African witchcraft);

•ancestral tradition (the field of the spirits related to the present settlement and the foundation of the community).[22]

Thus the *nganga*'s most significant task (because it touches on the "sacred" foundation of the community) is that of ensuring the harmonious coexistence of the village with the *simbi*, those spirits of the earth and water and other media, long since dead but active again, wandering among the living.[23]

Each time a new village is built or any important undertaking is planned, the traditional "chief of the land" calls on the *nganga* to ensure peace, prosperity, and continuity. At the site of a new village, the *nganga* will plant a branch brought from the old village and ask the *simbi* to accept and welcome the newcomers.

Everyone, of course, tries individually to live in peace with the dead (former occupants of the land, the original Ancestors, the first creatures). In Kongo country, in each hut or compound one finds *nkisi*, artifacts designed to subdue the invisible creatures of the African mesocosmos, constituting a veritable distillation of the

[22]"If the sorcerer is presented as a deviation from the social ideal and as the invasion of the individual and singular in the heart of social cohesion, the magician is defined as a constructor of society. His principal function is to do battle against sorcerers and sorcery and to destroy them" (Zahan, 1970, p. 102).

With Doutreloux (1967), one can make a distinction between good magic ("in the service of society and individuals, but without harming society") and the bad magic of sorcerers ("the art of destroying and devouring").

[23]The *simbi* (spirits) are forces/beings of the mesocosmos endowed with their own power. People believe that the *simbi* are displeased with them when their health fails, when disease or death strikes, or when discord develops.

laws of nature (made of finished products or materials taken directly from nature), evidence that the whole community is concerned with taming those "wild creatures," the *simbi,* with fixing them by giving them a tangible base.[24]

The *nganga,* however, is the only person capable of using, on his own, the power that is concentrated and invested in the *nkisi* object or carrier (the head of the family being merely its custodian). Charged with "capturing the *simbi,"* he traps and imprisons them, fixing them in the *nkisi;* when they get loose, he recovers them.[25] The *simbi,* or spirits, are a kind of personification of natural forces and laws; mastering them is a cultural feat whereby man appropriates them to his own ends.

An invisible presence, a concrete expression, living evidence — the *nkisi* is a fundamental working tool for the *nganga.* Beyond this symbol, however, beyond this intermediary device, there is a whole battery of genuinely therapeutic procedures:[26] "interventions...

[24]A *nkisi* is a point of conjunction, a place of contact between the *simbi* and men. It is a substitute for and symbolic representation of a *simbi* as an invisible force. *Simbi* and *nkisi* constitute a system of constraint or confinement for maintaining social order; they are a favored means for combating *ndoki* (sorcerers).

[25]Capturing the *simbi* consists of a veritable hunt in which everyone participates; it involves real group psychotherapy (with symbolic effectiveness).

[26]It is irrelevant that some of these procedures bear the stamp of the "group ideology." As Buakasa (1971) notes, the important thing is the efficacy of these practices: "Efficacy being the criterion... in so far as it permits a sense of security and confidence on the part of individuals in the means that society offers... the *kindoki* and the *nkisi* themselves, as a mode of knowledge, are of particular importance not because they are equivalent to a scientific treatise — far from it — but because they resolve certain problems that arise within the society" (p. 16).

growing out of a knowledge of remedies and rituals that purportedly make it possible to act on the forces considered responsible for suffering" (Buakasa, 1971, p. 13). For suffering (sickness, misfortune) is always caused by "natural forces."

The very term *nganga* evokes competence, cleverness, ingenuity, know-how.[27] The *nganga* is the one who can do the job when it is a question of ensuring the health of the body, the fecundity of women, the fertility of the fields (consequently, he is often physician, obstetrician, agronomist, all in one). He is the doer of good who seeks to check the destructive will of the *ndoki* (natural forces: his opposites and complements).[28] Usually both diagnostician and therapist,[29] he is:

1. *nganga ngambo,* he who seeks the source of the sickness (diagnostician), who discovers and denounces the *ndoki;*[30] and

2. *nganga buka* or *nganga nkisi,* he who cares for the *mbevo* (the sick person).[31]

---

[27]Hence the use of the term in other contexts, e.g., the priest of Nzambi (the supreme God) is called "*nganga* Nzambi."

[28]The *nganga-ndoki* pair, (i.e., healing-harmful) has its equivalent in every African society: for example, *wulumo-kuino* among the Kissi (Paulme, 1954), *suman-bayifo* among the Ashanti (Rattray, 1927), *shanty-tyarkaw* among the Songhai (Rouch, 1960). The sorcerer takes the side of the bad, of night, of destruction; the healer-practitioner belongs to the good, to light, to what is constructive and social.

[29]"Specialist, expert, skilled in conducting searches to discover and denounce the source of sickness or in caring for *mbevo,*" i.e., those who are sick (Buakasa, 1971, p. 272).

[30]The *nganga-ngombo* or *nganga-manga* is a specialist whose function (in sessions called *vuela, zalala, ngombo,* or *manga)* is to give instructions concerning the conditions of cure, after having identified the causes of the sickness.

[31]The *nganga nkisi* takes prophylactic action on behalf of individuals against any threat.

The technical skill he acquires during initiation *(bunda-nkisi* = manipulation of the *nkisi* and the *simbi)* is employed primarily in the field of physical medicine. Assisted by his *nkisi* and by aides (students) in the exercise of his functions, he cares for a clientele that is sometimes very large, and that knows of his abilities in the areas of prevention and treatment and even surgery (in this connection see Janzen, 1969).

A *nganga* often specializes according to the particular *nkisi* (and hence the spirit or natural force responsible for a certain ailment) with which he happens to be associated. Thus a *nganga* may declare himself unqualified to treat a certain type of disorder, in which case he refers his client to a colleague whom he considers a competent specialist.[32]

His psychotherapeutic and sociotherapeutic skills are no less impressive. The *nganga* knows that sickness can be initially caused (or furthered) by festering relations between members of the patient's lineage; unable to do anything without the support of the kin, he may get them to discuss their problems and/or make peace with one another publicly. Public debate can have a cathartic effect.[33] The *nganga* should take advantage of the situation; it is an opportunity to provide reassurance and restore confidence while strengthening social bonds, a time of understanding and solidarity. By facilitating the dramatic discharge of aggressiveness in this way, aggressiveness caused by the frustration of unfulfilled

---

[32]Patients go from one *nganga* to another, depending on the *nganga*'s specialty, or on whether or not he has given satisfaction.

[33]The *nganga* brings the members of the family together and asks them to say aloud what they are harboring deep down inside.

needs or desires, he settles interpersonal differences and resolves social discord.

The healer is unquestionably much closer to his peers than the diagnostician is; rooted more in the community, the healer acts openly, in the broad light of day, in no way seeking to conceal the power of his knowledge (cf. Junod, 1912, vol. 2, p. 452ff.). Yet he is an uncontested master of the public stage; he polarizes the group's tendencies and interests (he has always played an important political role in the broad sense). Certain insignia, attributes of his rank and social status, symbolize a power that complements that of political leaders.[34]

In Kongo country, the *nganga's* costume consisted of a close-fitting knitted one-piece suit. He wore a clay mask and a headdress, with long brown raffia fringe covering his shoulders and chest. The mask was smeared with a reddish brown coating.

Among the Yoruba in Nigeria, *babalaos* used to carry a Shango staff, a wooden cylinder surmounted by a Janus head from which sprang two large pointed flanges representing bolts of lightning, a symbol of the power of thunder and light. This staff also served as scepter for the king and for priests. It was reputed to provide protection against sterility and epidemics.

The initiation of a future healer is far more than a course of familiarization with diseases and their treat-

---

[34]Wing (1921) reports that any notable preparing to assume an important position used to go through a long retreat with the *nganga*, in order to acquire protection against any grudges his rivals might harbor against him. If the *nganga* once played a political role, conversely, great political leaders, along with legendary and historical heroes, were credited with a power beyond the ordinary, consistent with their responsibilities.

ment; it consists first and foremost of familiarization with the surrounding world, with the human beings, animals, and plants of the microcosmic world, but also with the invisible natural forces (genies, spirits) of the mesocosmic world.[35] The initiator takes the neophyte into the bush during his initiation in order to bring him face to face with beings and things, which in essence is also a way of bringing him face to face with himself, for being able to "stick it out" through initiation in the bush is in itself already evidence of personal strength. The pupil will learn to identify the special places where the forces of nature are deployed, their various manifestations, and their ceaseless activity in space (land, sky, and water). Similarly, he will develop his senses for keen and careful observation of natural phenomena (the seasonal cycles, the rain and the wind, the movement of heavenly bodies). He will acquire a knowledge of botany, agriculture, geology, and the like, as well as religious training. In sum, then, initiation frequently amounts to the basic training (common to all initiated adults) of the future traditional practitioner.

If this retreat into the heart of living nature provides the future practitioner an opportunity for acquiring positive knowledge, it nevertheless also remains a supervised apprenticeship in the mastery of his own person-

[35]"The battle against sorcerers depends on a knowledge and technique that the magician acquires by initiation, that is, through a progressive unveiling of things conducted simultaneously with the opening up of the mind and intellect. This latter step is often integrated into profoundly religious rites which touch upon the mystical life. However, what is important in practical terms in this period of formation, is the neophyte's initiation into the manipulation of symbols and into the logic concerning the relations between things" (Zahan, 1970, p. 103).

ality, both from the individual standpoint and from the interpersonal, social, cultural, moral, and mystical points of view. It is understood that initiation is the surest way of acquiring a place of esteem in community life. When he rejoins the group, the future practitioner's position is enhanced because of his experience and knowledge, which are all the more prestigious in that they are not "common."[36]

With respect to acquiring fundamental knowledge in a narrower sense, the future practitioner learns to distinguish the three basic etiological registers that are the three major realms or areas of dynamic conflict:

1. Tradition — ancestry (the realm of vertical relations);

2. Synchrony (the realm of horizontal relations, i.e., the area of social experience);

3. The more restricted family (the realm of intrafamilial relations).

It is this fundamental subdivision that gives rise to the variety of practices and hence to the specialization of practitioners.[37] The future practitioner is instructed in the various causes and forms of disease,[38] and as his knowledge deepens with day-to-day experience, he may

[36]The practitioner's "secret" consists of a vivid experience, intensely felt but hard to communicate. It lies in the real and progressively integrated fullness of a personality that is methodically reconstructed with the most fundamental elements of the native culture.

[37]And ultimately, after this acquisition of fundamentals, to a more marked specialization of certain initiation programs.

[38]Though the search for causes (and thereby meaning) is fundamental, learning about symptoms is not neglected. In the absence of treatises on anatomy, sometimes sculpture fills an important role; in masks one finds numerous physical indications of disease (including epilepsy and insanity) — for example in the masks of the Ekpo society of the Ibibio in Nigeria.

(like any medical student) develop a more specific specialty, consistent with greater experience concerning one of the realms or fields of dynamic conflict defined above.

Among the Mundang, any healer is called *pa-sinri*, that is, he who "possesses" and administers medicines. But in discussing diseases or seeking diagnoses, every therapist is referred to in terms of his particular competence and the nature of the *sinri* he possesses. To cite but a few, the *pa-fa-masan-li* is he who possesses and controls *(pa)* things *(fa)*, i.e., medicines and therapeutic procedures, that enable him to cure sickness *(masan-li)*. The *pa-fa-sak* possesses secrets and *sinri* that equip him to combat sorcery. The *pa-fa-cox-sinri* specializes in treating seizures provoked by local genies. The *pa-fa-tagware-dobfu* appeases the *tagware* of the dead. All of these healers, who are often former sufferers of the illness they specialize in treating, work individually. They form no corporate body or society, and once treatment has ended they do not maintain any special relationship with their erstwhile patients (Adler and Zempleni, 1972, p. 86).

It is through contact with a master, to whom a student is bound by an unbreakable contract,[39] that the novice acquires the requisite technical knowledge to make diagnoses and provide treatment.[40] During

[39]The postulant pays the initiator; he may make an agreement binding himself to him, entering into a covenant with him.

[40]Sometimes medical knowledge is passed from father to son. The healer's family is then alone in holding the secrets concerning certain ills and their remedies (according to Zahan, 1970, pp. 102–103, this is the most common way of acquiring medical knowledge).

consultations (which usually take place in the evening or at night, sometimes at the home of the patient), the assistant learns to read "the signs of sickness" and combat them (or possibly prevent them).

Numerous courses of pharmacological and psychotherapeutic action are available to the therapist, methods that have consistently proved to be efficacious. Thus the candidate is trained to handle an array of medicines and even to perform a variety of interventions (amputation, suturing, bleeding, etc.). Technical competence, however, is never enough for an African practitioner. The aim of training is always to combine knowledge with know-how and to relate it to the anthropological universe as a whole. Therefore, for the Kongo *nganga* of Zaïre (Buakasa, 1971), mere knowledge of the properties of plants and herbs is insufficient unless treatment is supplemented, supported, and preceded by the ritual of their administration.[41]

Whatever the affliction being treated, gestures and words also have their value during therapeutic sessions with the *nganga*. Organized and established as rituals, used under very specific conditions of time and place, the formulas that are recited, the chants and invocations, make up a language of secret symbolism in which the word influences the *simbi* (spirits, natural forces); moreover, they activate and strengthen the therapeutic action of the medicines. Considered separately, it is not

[41]Substances are not gathered just any day, prepared no matter how, and administered no matter when. Ritual (a symbolic system of words, acts, signs, and signifiers) representing the original fundamental deed is intended to recreate it and so do away with misfortune and usher in good fortune.

always easy to interpret them; but on the other hand, to interpret them properly, a whole study would have to be devoted to each formulation, detailing the history of the community, its legends and vicissitudes, as well as all the sociocultural components of the present life.

Various behaviors that are decreed or prohibited (in regard to sex and food) are standards imposed on the practitioner,[42] mainly with a view to demonstrating self-control before any attempt is made to solve the conflicts of others.[43] In other words the practitioner's personal cleanliness must precede and prepare the way for any action of social importance. In Black Africa, those who undergo a long initiation often acquire experience, a personality, and psychological qualities that unquestionably have a favorable and beneficial effect on their patients.

Diviners and healers. . .have often been judged

---

[42]In a similar vein, strict ethical principles dictate that a practitioner be remunerated only if he provides satisfaction.

[43]Taboos cannot at base be considered outside the cultural context of which they are an integral part. Nothing can be postulated outside that context. Still, that does not explain taboos; it is simply a reference system, rich to be sure, that organizes them, in terms of the therapeutic practice in question here, into a system functioning in an autonomous manner, that is, into an agency having its own structure and its own internal laws of organization. The history that gave rise to this practice may be forgotten in time, lost in the depths of man's mind. Beyond these references, in such taboos are seen notions not formulated in thought, projections of the unconscious, of the invisible, which are obscured by the cultural context.

At the level of the individual, taboos ensure the efficacy of the *nkisi*, guaranteeing their protection.

In terms of analyzing the phenomenon, taboos are a matter of tradition and therefore call for respect in that, strictly speaking, they consist of learning the common law essential to every community, beyond onself and one's own wishes, incumbent upon all.

incorrectly, as have fetishes and so-called secret societies. All these traditional features formed part of the tribal social framework, on the same level as religion. They moderated the wildness of youth, spread the art of midwifery and the techniques of hunting and fishing, as well as showed the course to follow in case of accident. Their ill-considered repression has often led to chaos and done more harm than good [P. Huard, cited in Sonolet, 1971, p. 19].

Although therapeutic techniques are combined (they may be used simultaneously or successively, and there is no really sharp distinction between purely physical and purely psychological treatment), it is possible to differentiate various categories of therapists in every African society; the diagnosticians, as well as the patients themselves, usually know what type of healer should be entrusted with a given type of illness. This multiplicity of practitioners is accompanied, it must be added, by a hierarchy of expertise and by competition that is sometimes very keen (instances of collaboration between specialists are not rare, however).

At the bottom of the scale are no doubt the herbalists (e.g., the *borom rem* or "root men" among the Wolof and Lebu of Senegal); serving as both pharmacists and healers, they personally concoct their remedies (laxatives, diuretics, ointments, plasters) and sell them in the markets. They have at their disposal a wide range of plants, which they use in preparations that are administered in various ways (by swallowing, rubbing, bathing, etc.). Purveyors of various powders, plants, and barks, they sometimes travel very far while vending their products. For instance, the Hausa *boka* are itinerant doctors whose aphrodisiacs, in particular, are touted throughout West Africa.

The purely technical and pharmacological values of this elementary medicine, which stress the economic side of the patient-practitioner relationship, are undeniable. And yet, as Monfouga-Nicolas (1972) points out, the somewhat mercantile character of this relationship "ends up by strengthening the medicine's psychological effect: the more expensive it is, the more efficacious it is. The placebo effect always seems evident, whether it be total (if the 'medicine' is absolutely worthless in itself) or whether it only strengthens a medicine already active on its own" (p. 67).

Some of these "medicine men" are frequently also "witch-finders," magicians who employ amulets and talismans (e.g., the *biledjo,* among the Peul and Wolof of Senegal, who are responsible for combating the *doem* or nocturnal evildoers). In their therapeutic armory they possess paraphernalia whose symbolism would be interesting to trace in detail — objects of animal origin (tails and horns, fish scales, lion claws and fangs, hyena teeth, bird skulls, shells, etc.), vegetable matter (powders), mineral and human substances (bones, hair, including facial and body hair, nail parings, skulls). Worn by individuals (on the arm, around the neck, on the breast, around the hips), such talismans protect the wearers, playing a substantial (prophylactic) psychological role (cf. Lehmann and Memel Foté, 1967, pp. 114–115).[44]

[44]These magic protectors serve as assurance against the dangers of life, as

As in any well-structured and cohesive society, "preventive procedures frequently outnumber curative procedures. The talismans worn by children, and by men and women as well, are as numerous as they are varied" (Monfouga-Nicolas, 1972, p. 68).

There is always a certain ambiguity regarding the status of witch-finders, which is evident in the ambivalence with which Africans perceive them. In effect, the whole business is a matter of nocturnal magic and activities, clandestine, so it is hard to distinguish between the good and the bad, and in any event one can easily go from one to the other. Witch-finder and witch share the same shadowy world. As Paulme (1954) reports of the Kissi of the Guinea forest, the *wulumo* (witch-finder) is identified with the *kuino* (witch):

> Public opinion does not contest the beneficent role of the witch-finder: the *wulumo* combats a public danger, "the witch is the enemy of all." But the idea of such a struggle seems no less suspect: how...would the witch-finder recognize witches and how would he combat them if he himself were not initiated into their secrets — if he himself were

---

Holas (1948) and Silla (1967) have pointed out in connection with the *tere* and the *galaty*, amulets that are worn by Senegalese.

Sometimes the practitioner himself is bedecked with numerous objects or articles of clothing intended not only to differentiate him but to protect him against the forces he has to deal with. According to Amon d'Aby (1960), "it is essential that he be able, on the one hand, to provide the patients entrusted to him protection from attack and, on the other hand, to defend himself from the evil fate his enemies are bound to will upon him. It happens, in fact, that, by way of reprisal, sorcerers may try to harm a healer who has restored the health of their victim" (p. 53).

not a *kuino*, a killer and eater of human flesh [pp. 288–289]?

As opposite poles within himself, the magician can embody the complex and contradictory aspects of knowledge: knowledge that relates to life and knowledge that relates to death. Magic (good) and sorcery or witchcraft (bad) are, as a matter of fact, two necessary complements of reality (their antagonism being manifested as opposition only at the level of discontinuity).[45]

In Islamic countries certain practitioners use deductive divination and fashion *tere*, protective amulets containing verses from the Koran, as well as brewing potions to defend body and mind against supernatural beings such as jinn and *seytane*.[46]

The late Abdoulaye Sadji (1955) has given us an excellent description:

> Among African marabouts and healers, holy water is a common prescription for preventing or curing, not physical ills at all, but the insidious and deadly effects caused by certain invisible creatures around us — jinn and sorcerers — interfering in our mental

[45]Zahan (1970) has aptly observed that "the existence of the individual and society is grasped on the social level in terms of opposition and undergoes the treatment befitting the elements of a linear series, whereas it is perceived on the deep level of existence in terms of conjunction and is subjected to the treatment befitting cyclical elements. In both cases we are concerned with death and life. . . . Any magician is potentially a sorcerer just as life is but a latent period of death" (p. 109).

[46]In Senegal the following are used for therapeutic purposes: writings in praise of the Prophet; systems of numbered tables and Arabic inscriptions (the names considered "powerful" are called *waindere*); suras and special prayers against the "Evil One"; ritual texts *(bakk* being appellations or mottoes; *dyat,* incantations; *lemu,* prayers); various substances having sacred connotations, e.g., sand from holy places, holy water, etc.

life. It is not easy to say by what process the holy
water that is concocted in diverse ways by masters
of the black art succeeds in dispelling all those constellations of impalpable beings, whose sole purpose seems to be to bring about in man a diminu-
tion of vitality and psychic equilibrium. Many people go off as raving lunatics after encountering at
night, under some dark and baleful tree, or in
broad day, in the center of a throbbing whirlwind,
the fatal smile of a jinni or the eye of a sorcerer,
eater of souls. In the fit of madness brought on by
such visions, they tear off their clothes, renounce
their membership in the caste of men, and discover
a new language which makes them taboo. Thenceforth a thick wall rises between them and us. And
they go off, dazed and in a trance, to conquer the
heavens where "those who seduced them" are
snickering. To bring them back to the humble fold
of man, holy water is needed, brewed from roots
and verses of the Koran, a holy water that drives
out all evil spells, exorcising any latent traces, that
restores to these victims of jinn or sorcerers their
normal personality and that social and human
ability to think and talk like everybody else.

Nevertheless, the status of certain marabouts is
similarly ambiguous and "borderline." They are both
revered and feared, especially those who engage in
black magic, also called "maraboutage," recalling the
"fétichage" of non-Moslem areas. Carried out at the request of clients, often in the form of complex games of
synchronous competition, it consists of attacking an

enemy or rival or neutralizing him through appropriate symbolic manipulations.

> Because of their understanding of botany, psychology, and human nature, because of their "power" which far exceeds their "knowledge," because of some of their therapeutic results, African healers deserve to be called doctors. For scientific medicine is too often content to treat somatic lesions without concerning itself with the fears and anxieties of the persons who are sick, whereas the healer worthy of that name considers the soul above all and always seeks to establish a climate of total confidence between his patient and himself.
>
> Popular African medicine merits closer study. In practical terms, its coexistence with Western medicine poses a problem that we know little about. As in tropical Asia, however, it is likely that coexistence of the two forms of medicine is, in certain cases, essential. The abrupt, forced, and mass elimination of healers by administrators, who are ill-informed or too imbued with Western superiority, does not seem, *a priori*, to be as desirable a measure as one might think at first glance [Sonolet, 1971, p. 25].

In many respects the African systems already meet the norms that have been recently introduced into the clinical theory of contemporary Western medicine (cf. Thomas and Luneau, 1975, p. 246):

•the dynamic conception of illness and relations between the outside and inside of the subject;

•the importance of the body and of the imaginary

and symbolic registers in the treatment of mental disorders;

•the social or rather group aspect of healing;

•the synthetic view of the individual (body-spirit, the
person inseparable from his environment).

The "royal road" of illness is frequently still the way
in which therapists come to their profession. In fact, in
many cases, sickness is a vividly experienced phenomenon comparable to initiation, a genuine learning experience. This is true in the case of possession; under the
direction of a group of former sufferers, the sick person
is induced to be initiated with a view to becoming a
practitioner in turn (specializing in the technique of
possession). We are dealing, here, with a medical practice; but independent of its strictly therapeutic aspect, it
is also a means of personal development (initiation into
cultural values). Yet one can see that in reality it is very
hard to draw the line between what clearly and distinct-
ly belongs to the medical domain and what is part of
human development. Seen in this light, it could be that
the best possible therapy is indicated prophylaxis, in the
sense of (preventive) construction of a coherent, well-
developed personality.

Possession techniques, which I shall merely outline
here, can be looked at in several ways:

1. As a strictly somatic manifestation, possession is
characterized by generalized paroxysms:

> A long shudder runs first through the arms and
> shoulders, rises through the neck, then reaches the
> face. The head bobs right and left. Trembling in-
> vades the whole body, the torso vibrates, the thighs

twitch and quiver. This state lasts several minutes; perspiration that beaded the temples now streams over the face. The breath is short; the eyes, at first fixed, now roll upwards. A sort of intoxication seems to come over the body, with a gradual loss of consciousness, a loss of awareness of what is going on round about [Monfouga-Nicolas, 1972, p. 177].[47]

2. As a psychological phenomenon, possession (fostered and/or triggered by music and hallucinogens)[48] consists of a convulsive mobilization of the deeper layers of the personality.

3. As a sociocultural phenomenon, this "critical" state, which in all cases is induced and controlled, is largely determined, in terms of its directly observable external manifestations (i.e., its overt aspects), by the cultural frame of reference of the person undergoing the crisis. Possession seems to be codified, contained within an institution;[49] the phenomenon is expressed in precise

[47]Monfouga-Nicolas (1972) continues: "After this series of incantations, the woman is literally exhausted. Her entire body is racked with pain, her muscles ache, she asks that someone stretch out her arms and legs. She remains recumbent for several hours in order to recover her physical and mental equilibrium" (pp. 178–179).

[48]Techniques of possession, though widespread, have been studied more thoroughly in certain ethnic groups (the Hausa, Songhai, Bariba, Fang, Mitsogo, etc.). It is known that hallucinogenic plants, such as Datura Mémel and Iboga Baillon, are used with great technical skill to induce the state of trance that precedes possession proper. Numerous studies have been devoted to this subject.

[49]Yet I refrain from speaking of a "possession cult." It is not a matter of the survival of some old animist cult (from the liturgical point of view), as Leroux (1948) contends; nor are the possessed therapists priests, even though they manipulate and are manipulated by invisible forces. And neither are they "mares of the gods."

socialized gestures, and, in fact, "chaotic, spontaneous manifestations, left solely to the subject's initiative, would be of no more than individual interest, with no social import" (Monfouga-Nicolas, 1972, p. 196). It could almost be described as a spectacle in which everyone is expected to take part, as actor or as spectator, within the forms and boundaries fixed by tradition. It is in this sense that:

> the body of a person possessed is a community affair; it is the stage in which a supernatural force concerning the village or family group manifests itself. This dramatic "take over" makes the "mad" body a spectacular pole, but the spectacle is controlled, ordered by the spectators themselves. . . .
>
> Far from being weakened or demeaned by the experience of madness, [the person possessed] becomes a touchstone for the group, a guide: his "difference," his uniqueness makes him a privileged person, that is, a person who is very free and at the same time very dependent, who has a less repressed, more extended body language but must place his own abilities at the service of the group, for he now knows how to make the Unconscious speak [Roche, 1972, p. 1061].

It may be helpful to outline, in simplified form, two broad types of possession (without ruling out intermediate modalities):

1. Possession that results in a "successful," controlled, transcendent experience in terms of individual and social conditions. From the practical and functional point of view, it is equivalent to initiation — a learning

experience that equips someone who benefits from it to eventually join the ranks of those who will be able to help others profit from what they have learned.

2. Possession that, because of various reasons or factors, amounts to an experience of failure, a sort of bungled, "unsuccessful" initiation, which results in mental trouble that "does not get better." This is one of the interpretations that may be given to certain chronic psychoses that drag on and on.

In regard to successful, initiatory possession, Zahan (1970) reports:

> The period of convalescence is also an initiatory period since, from the "invalid" he was until this point, the possessed person is transformed into a disciple of his healer. He accompanies the healer everywhere in his movements, helps him in cures, and is initiated into the art of exorcism. . . . From then on the formerly possessed person is completely changed in status. He belongs to the society of those who are capable of "manipulating" the world of the spirits [p. 148].

Initiatory possession, which is an integral part of the training for successful sociocultural experience, is socially sanctioned and not regarded as a pathological state. It is the business of "professionals." Thus it is organized, induced, and supervised by professional associations at the request of clients (e.g., the well-known Baki of Niger and Bwiti of Gabon). Such possession makes it possible to expand the dialogue with the depths of one's being — those depths being represented by invisible forces (which they are, moreover) — and, going on from there, to intervene on behalf of a private client or the community. Depending on the problem to be treated, a specialist is called on, dealing with a particular type of problem corresponding to the specialty of a given "genie."[50] The person possessed acts like a "mare" mounted by a rider.[51] The genies or forces that descended straddle the adept, take possession of his or her body, and temporarily take the place of the subject's personality, yet without destroying it. During the phase of possession proper, the possessed "specialist" is questioned by the master technician in the field of trance and possession, and it is then that answers are given to the specific questions that motivated the organization of the trance-possession séance. When questioned, the genie (subconscious-unconscious) replies through the mouth of the person possessed, making the diagnosis and suggesting solutions for settling the conflict.

[50]Genies are spirits representing obscure forces of the traditional structured world of the collective imaginary. At the community as well as the individual level, they portray realities, personified by the culture, of what might be compared to the Freudian subconscious-unconscious system. In any case, the mesocosmos, the realm of genies (doubles of men), is also the realm of desires and fears.

[51]I have been able to verify, personally, that in Niger the Bori professional — who, apart from his or her work, is a man or woman who differs little from anyone else — is called "the genie's horse," to be precise. In the interest of accuracy, I am regretfully obliged, despite the bonds of personal friendship, to refute the title assigned to such specialists by Monfouga-Nicolas, namely, "mares of the gods." The fact is, the Bori professional has nothing to do with the gods, and even less with the question of divinity in Africa. The supposed pantheon described by Monfouga-Nicolas (1972) is in no sense a pantheon. What it concerns, after all, are those beings of the traditional mesocosmos: genies (the term that seems most appropriate to designate them), whose society is a replica — structured, invisible, and of course "powerful" — of human society (mythical twins of men and women). Nor are these beings worshipped in any truly religious sense, as is clear from the Hausa myth that Monfouga-Nicolas herself has reported elsewhere.

It can be said that a well-ordered séance, organized by professionals and following a strict scenario of possession, constitutes real-life theater in the full sense of the term, as one finds among the Songhai of Niger as well as the Ethiopians of Gondar, the Fon of Dahomey, the Yoruba and Hausa of Nigeria, etc. The theatrical and psychodramatic qualities of these public sessions, with a cast of professional players attuned to the real-life culture, promote catharsis, the discharge of tensions, and the resolution of conflicts. One may rightly speak of genuine psychodrama.[52]

Against that background, possession as a successful personal achievement is a scenario on which we should focus our attention. It constitutes a type of apprenticeship, training in the functions of diagnostic support, and paves the way for accession later on to the highly desirable status of diagnostician proper, as a master who will direct and interrogate the deep psychic layers of his fellow experts in trance-possession.

But not every sick person who experiences possession is inevitably called on to become a therapist (and, conversely, not every therapist has necessarily been sick, even though he must have experienced possession to be initiated into diagnostic and healing practices). It is important to understand that only a restricted number of

[52]In organized possession séances, there is a dance master who ushers in one or more associates in a state of trance-possession; he himself remains lucid and conscious, however, for his role is that of diagnostician, while his colleagues in a state of trance serve as diagnostic vehicles or instruments. It is the deep layers of their psychic system that then "speak." Through them, in a nonconscious state, the collective imaginary, the source of troubles, is what is questioned. The traditional imaginary is a structured imaginary.

patients are actually initiated, that is, only a few are ultimately chosen as future colleagues by the practicing therapists. Selection of a patient is governed by closely related psychological and sociological criteria, notably the subject's personality and the social milieu to which he belongs. As Monfouga-Nicolas (1972, p. 95) has noted, there are clearly "Bori families," but without, in this particular case, any question of inheritance entering the picture.

Thus a threefold set of conditions — physiological, sociological, psychological — is at the base of a patient's accession to the rank of initiate; the individual's total personality is involved — in its sociological dimensions through environmental influences, in its physiological dimensions through illness, and in its psychological dimensions as a result of personal factors (Monfouga-Nicolas, 1972, p. 99).

Together, these conditions qualify a patient to embark on the long process that, by bringing sickness (evil) under control, leads to harmony: initiation represents a genuine active passage, a bridge that is built, a course that is "conquered," from nature to civilization, from the chaotic to the coherent in terms of the values giving the greatest structure to the person/personality.

Initiation with the art of possession, which may vary considerably in form and duration from one ethnic group to another, is in essence a matter of:

•becoming conscious of the social importance and cultural significance of the deep layers of the psychic system (the collective imaginary bound up with the pole of ancestral symbols and represented by genies or spirits);

•acquiring mastery of one's overall personal economy as well as of techniques that assure its deployment at the three levels of the real, the imaginary, and the symbolic.[53]

But also, on a more technical level, such initiation is a matter of:

•coming to recognize the agents of aggression (identifying the malevolent beings of the mesocosmos);

•learning the remedies that cure, at the purely somatic level;

•learning to implement socially oriented treatment techniques.

As an example, let us take initiation among the Songhai of Niger as reported by Rouch (1960), an example that can be expanded, moreover, to include the phenomenon among the Hausa (also in Niger) studied by Monfouga-Nicolas (1972).

For days at a time great seizures rack those who have been chosen as mares by the *holey*, or spirits, making it essential to call in the *zima* (master of the *holey* and dance master of the adepts). Only he has the skill to pacify the possessing spirits, to control them. He puts others in a state of trance and watches closely what develops. In the form of litanies, he chants the spirits' names; he conducts ceremonies to honor them; and (like

---

[53]Coherent articulation of these three levels (real, imaginary, and symbolic) describes, precisely, culture in action. The essential problem, in any living culture, is to find out how "imaginary" themes that develop turn into "symbols," and then how symbolic constructs come to act effectively in the practical social reality of everyday — or to put it another way, how these three fundamental levels of total human reality are structured and ordered in a given society, in view of all the risks there are of minimizing one level or another.

the *sohantye*, the healer-magician) he prepares *safari*, or medicines, against the *tyarkaw* who steal man's mind. He is also, first and foremost, the initiator and instructor of adepts in the technique of possession.

Initiation, which takes place in three phases, transforms the sick person into a *holey bari*, that is, a "possession dancer" or adept. Among the Songhai, initiation does not consist of driving out or exorcising the spirit but of "taking it on, accepting it, delivering body and soul to it for a period of apprenticeship" (Heusch, 1965, p. 149). Chaos becomes order, silence becomes speech:

First phase (fimbyon): the sick person is "shaken" until the spirit possessing him is identified (the *zima*, a veritable stage director and master of ceremonies, should know whether it is a case of an ordinary *holey* and should be able to name it, or rather make it reveal its name).

Second phase (gumandi): the spirit, whom the subject is getting to know, is pacified thanks to the intervention of the *holey ize* (musicians) and the *holey kongo* (soothing women), who lavish attention on the patient, mothering him, in the hut where he is temporarily isolated for two or three days.

Third phase (ganandi): the patient revives, then learns the steps of the dance technique that enables the *holey* to manifest themselves (at the *zima's* command); both a rite of passage and a rite of integration, the *ganandi*, which may last for two weeks and sometimes takes place years after the *gumandi* phase, marks the real beginning of actual technical apprenticeship to the position of practitioner (which is restricted to *holey bari* whose capacities have been tested by the *zima*).

The initial "sickness' has thus been put right (a personal experience that has been carried off well), transformed first into a communication structure and then into a system of overt action on the community.

One may compare the initiation of the *holey bari* with that of the *borom rab* in Senegal (literally, the *rab* or spirit possessors), which also takes place in a series of major phases and in similar circumstances:

1. Preparing for and achieving the "possession seizure" proper: sprinkling with water and milk, invocation of the spirits, massaging, mothering, descent of the *rab* or spirit, identification of the spirit.

2. *Bukotu:* symbolic death and rebirth; *fetia* (dances); *rey* (sacrifices); *samp* (setting up the *khamb* or "trap" for spirits).

3. *Ratya* training (several days after installation of the *khamb*): dances marking the official entry of the former *lefohar* into the ranks of the *borom rab*.

4. Learning therapeutic actions, being initiated to the *bak* (songs and chants of the great *tur*).

> The individual finds himself given the privileged status of intermediary between men and the spirits; this position is attained only after initiation into a series of gestures and dances; psychomotor actions are learned with the help of the *ndoepkat*, women who act as veritable coaches in bodily expression [Roche, 1972, p. 1061].

The therapeutic groupings that care for the afflicted under the direction of a master professional are structured, hierarchical groupings; each member holds a particular rank, commensurate with his or her abilities, that is, with the degree of initiation.[54]

In Senegal, among the Wolof and the Lebu (cf. Silla, 1967), the *kör* are veritable brotherhoods or families of specialists, corresponding to the *rab* and *tur* of lineages, clans, neighborhoods, and villages.[55] There may be several associations in the same village. Though the *kör* is an initiatory association, it is not a closed, secret society. Far from being recluses, its members participate normally in community life, apart from their therapeutic activities. They may be recruited from any social group.

After having gone through the experience of induced possession and trance, they turn their attention to the study of pharmacology, to the interpretation of symbols, to learning the psychodramatic procedures for combating *doem* (sorcerers), to acquiring a knowlege of ancestral traditions and practices, and, in particular, to constructing the space or site for fixing the *rab* and bringing them under control. As I have repeatedly pointed out, the crux of the matter is to learn to detect, then to fix, to master, and to manipulate, the dark forces of man (represented by genies or spirits), that is, the subconscious-unconscious complex.

A strict discipline generally governs the conduct of the healers, who are obedient to the *borom tur* (the chief of the group, as it were) and to the *borom rab bu mag* (the high counselor, who, along with the chief, settles questions of primary importance to the association).

---

[54]Sometimes also with degree of consanguinity (e.g., in the case of uterine transmission of *ndoepkat* capacities among the Wolof).

[55]A *rab* represents the link with ancestral traditions; when it is identified, named, "trapped," and fixed, it becomes a *tur* (the great *tur* are the original *rab*). There are certain "wandering" *rab* that cause madness.

Formerly officiating at agrarian rites, today the *borom tur* serves as *faty kat* (therapist), *borom ren* (herbalist), and *ndoepkat (ndoep* master), occupying the highest rung in the therapeutic hierarchy. He analyzes the wishes of the *tur*, displaying his diagnostic power (a power he shares with the *borom xam-xam*, an outstanding master of diagnostic skill). He acts as intermediary between the *tur* and the village, clan, or lineage. People look to him for rain and for prosperity; he is the source of fecundity and fertility. He is able to obtain responses from the world of unseen psychic forces to the questions put by his patients, and so he prescribes remedies (which he buys or concocts) and deciphers and transmits injunctions from the mesocosmos (the structured collective imaginary). His functions earn him an audience in the affairs of his village or town quarter.

The *ndoepkat*, chosen by a *rab*, knows how to stand up to *doem* (witches or sorcerers), to jinn (a variety of spirits, and to *nit ku bon*.[56] At the cost of a long initiation (lasting 20 years at times) he acquires a body of knowledge that qualifies him for his curative task (see also Zempleni, 1968).

Silla (1967) reports:

> The *ndoepkat* stand out by their behavior, which can be characterized as strange, bizarre, not normal for the society. They live "above" society, as it were, secluding themselves with the *khamb* (places

[56]The term *nit ku bon* designates both an agent of aggression ("the person who is bad") and a complex childhood syndrome resembling clinical autism, but without being so with respect to social and psychopathological state.

for fixing wandering spirits, dark and evil psychic
forces). They are distinguished by special attire: a
garish patchwork of clothing covering the whole
body. They set themselves apart from the profane
world in order to enter into communication with
the invisible world of the *rab* and the jinn [p. 165].

That world is the mesocosmos — a duplicate of the visible world, a place of fears and desires.

The *ndoepkat*[57] is assisted by initiates during public
séances of possession and trance. The *borom tur* are
more specifically responsible for the physical organization of a session (forming the corps of *ndoep* dancers,
these women take care of the patient, mother him,
coach him, dress him, look after him) and for
psychological assistance (they help calm the patient,
lavish attentions on him), whereas the *borom rab*
(possessed women who have been cured) — equivalent
to the adepts of the Songhai Hausa Bori — lend their
bodies willingly to the spirits and enter into a trance to
help bring about the release of the patient.[58]

---

[57]The equivalent in the Hausa Bori is the *uwal saye*, root mother and initiation mother, who knows the secrets of plants and barks, and has special ties to the spirits.

[58]The equivalent in the Hausa Bori is the *jakeso*, who takes care of the initiate. Serving neither as therapists nor as possessed, griots or musicians are indispensable auxiliaries: without them, no one would become possessed, for they alone have the power to summon the spirits. They therefore effectively second the therapists.

N.B.: It is very likely that such practices as the *ndoep* rituals and the Bori cult, along with the techniques of possession and trance, may originally have borne a feminine, maternal coefficient and have been related to the earth, fertility, fecundity, motherhood, and birth. It is not far-fetched to suggest, at least as a hypothesis, that all those practices and techniques may be "maternal" if not in origin at least in their underlying nature. In this

Both categories of women enjoy the esteem of the entire Lebu-Wolof community. Respect for their position obliges them to observe various taboos of a purifying nature (sexual continence) and to perform rituals intended to preserve their power and their resistance to attack from malevolent spirits (before any dangerous or important undertaking, ablutions are performed with water in which roots have been steeped from plants having both symbolic and pharmacodynamic properties). In order to reinforce the climate of solidarity, strict protocol also governs relations between various members of the institution.

The practical aspect of their activity (at the individual and social levels) does not lessen the cosmic import of the phenomenon of possession. Any treatment sessions is, at the same time:

1. a situation of privileged dialogue between the practitioner and the patient, between the practitioner and the genie or spirit, and between the patient and the genie or spirit, with all of these individual contacts being ordered according to an interrelational system;[59]

2. a situation of profound communication on the part of the therapists, as a body, with the invisible beings of the mesocosmos, which is experienced by the group as a cathartic, and genuinely curative, drama;

3. a situation of total interpenetration (between

---

sense, taking care of persons manifesting profound regression (psychotic or not) is, at base, more a "matter for mothers."

[59]The simple relationship between a pharmacist-practitioner and a patient (a vendor-buyer relationship) is distinguished from the relationship between a therapist and someone possessed (which recalls, in certain respects, the mother-child relationship); in the latter case, the contacts are close, repeated, and friendly (mothering — security).

microcosm, mesocosm, and macrocosm, on the one hand, and within the microcosm, on the other hand) through which the community recovers the well-being it had temporarily lost.

Providing care under the direction of "genies," which are the personification of deep psychic layers (invisible doubles of men who know all secrets), successfully performing their role as psychotherapists by serving as "mares," and keeping in their everyday life the ever-present potential to communicate with those invisible psychic forces, women therapists live and breathe communication between the visible and the invisible. Their role is therefore fundamental in societies caught up in perpetual internal evolution, in which people are confronted with the problems not only of expanding the restricted framework of the village or lineage community, but also, and especially, of harmoniously combining new values and thoroughly integrating them with the most vital sources of ancestral tradition (cf. Lombard, 1967).

Certain practitioners (so-called "prophets" of new messianic religions), who do not quite fit into the category of "traditional" — for example, Albert Atcho of the Ivory Coast — work individual or collective cures by using, in particular, the method of conversion and personal confession. Thousands of devotee-clients come to consult Atcho from all corners of the Ivory Coast.

Although the efficacy of therapeutic groups is rooted in rural environments, they seem to be proliferating in urban centers (as I indicated in Chapter 1).

The theoretical bases of traditional techniques and therapies, as construed from the findings of interdisciplinary research, will enable a developing Africa to evolve a style of therapeutic relations that is modern yet in harmony with dynamic African thinking and the African personality. It is essential to preserve the continuity between the social world, with its conflicts, and psychological or psychopathological problems, and to develop therapeutic services organized by established groups, while maintaining the highly social nature of the vocation — as opposed to a purely technical, analytical, and elitist character — for future African practitioners.

CHAPTER THREE

Outline of the Principal
Sociocultural Reference Systems
Concerning Experience of Self
in the Traditional Community

In this chapter, I do not propose to examine African anthropological structures in their own right. Despite the hundreds of studies on the subject that have already been published, it seems that the task of inventorying existing anthropological materials is still far from complete; *a fortiori*, we are in no position to embark on a spectral analysis with any pretensions of being exhaustive

The problems that confront us remain fundamentally the same: What major reference systems, what basic frameworks, what formative patterns can a psychiatrist glean from current knowledge in an effort to understand the points of articulation of the African person/personality in terms of a comprehensive psychiatric perspective? The reader, then, should expect to find no more than rough anthropological outlines from the hand of a nonspecialist.

Having said that, I would like to point out that the Black Africa we have been discussing thus far occupies, from the geographical and human point of view, almost the entire sub-Saharan portion of the African continent, which gives it a seemingly great polymorphism, at least at first glance:

•geographic diversity, evidenced by a variety of landscapes and climates;

•human diversity, which physical anthropology describes in terms of ethnic groups (Sudanic Negroes, Guineans, Congolese, Nilotes, Southern and Eastern Africans, Negrillos, Khoisan, Ethiopians);

•linguistic diversity (between 700 and 1,500 languages);

•religious diversity (traditional religions and the imported religions of Christianity and Islam);

•diversity of material civilization (leading Murdock, 1959, to isolate as many as 850 societies), along with diversity of lifestyle (sedentary and nomadic), production mode, and economic systems.[1]

---

[1]Maquet (1962) distinguishes the following categories: the civilizations

And yet, as Leo Frobenius contended at the beginning of the century, and as the originators of the ideas of "Africanity" or *"négritude"* have argued since, there does exist a certain unity among the traditional cultures of Black Africa, a unity that is evident in the realm of spirituality as well as in that of representation and expression, from works of art to behaviors manifested in everyday life.

This Negro-African culture (one need only refer to the hundreds of works devoted to it by scholars throughout the world) has still scarcely begun to be studied systematically and thoroughly in all its dimensions — historical, social, anthropological[2] — and yet what seems to emerge from all the writings is the degree of cultural homogeneity in Black Africa. There is no doubt that, with a few variations, African thought has a distinctive character, deriving its principles from symbols and myths (merging into one the universe and the society in which the African person/personality is formed) as well as from a collective ritual (permitting precise location of the individual in relation to his environment and to the course of his development).

It is impossible to think of African psychology and, *a fortiori*, African psychopathology without reference to the anthropological structures of the sense of self in the various stages of traditional life:

•On the one hand, in Africa the person is not a closed

---

of the bow (hunting-gathering), of the clearings (forest agriculture), of the granaries (savanna agriculture), of the spear (pastoralist and warrior societies), of cities, and of industry.

   [2]Cf. Ki-Zerbo, 1972. In the last 15 years, a few dozen doctoral dissertations have focused on Black Africa.

system, standing against the outside world; there, more markedly than elsewhere, the individual cannot be thought of except in close relation with everything around him — an environment filled with cultural signifiers in a universe that is itself panstructured.

•On the other hand, the African person/personality is not a "completed" system (already at three to five years of age); the human being, as such, is perpetually "in the making." From the psychological and psychopathological point of view, difficulties and conflicts are always present, seen in a context of ceaseless development, for the personality is continually evolving in a life that is felt to unfold in an orderly fashion, dominated, at its highest point, by the ideas of seniority and ancestry. The basic stages or phases of life (codified through rituals and traditional practices, including initiation) permit progressive integration into a well-ordered universe (because it has not been stripped of its fundamental signifiers), having a high symbolic content. The status of full person is really acquired only with old age, which takes on an ancestral quality.

Inseparable from his social dimensions, the individual in Africa (from an analytical point of view) appears composite in space, multiple in time, extending and testifying to a culture of rich complexity (cf. Jahn, 1958). Only an anthropological perspective that views the personality as a living system of social relations and a system of interaction with the realm of the symbolic will enable one to grasp the way in which Africans experience the self.

The concept of person sums up and brings together the ideas and principles of traditional Negro-African thought. Indeed, one finds there the necessity of pluralism, the networks of participation and correspondence that bind the subject to the group and to the cosmos, the verbal dimensions, the dynamic and unfinished quality, the richness and the fragility, the important role assigned to the milieu, and the inevitable reference to the sacred [Thomas and Luneau, 1975, p. 27].

Anthropologists surveying Africa today, call attention not only to the variety and richness of the traditional religious symbols but also to the remarkable uniformity of belief and the dominantly monotheistic character of religious thought.[3]

All African peoples are basically religious, and they share the concept of one God as creator, omnipotent and omnipresent. It has been proved, moreover, that this idea well antedates the importation of the Islamic and Judeo-Christian religions; furthermore, it is a central point in the themes of the great foundation myths. Monotheism is found in the thought systems of even the smallest African groups.[4]

---

[3]There is no need to dwell on this point here, for today, as yesterday, it is incontestable.

[4]According to Amon d'Aby (1960), "Even before any contact with people of the white race, the Agni had formed the idea of the existence of one supreme God, the creator of men, animals, and things. The Sanwi call this supreme God Alluko-Nyamia-Kadyes; the Baule, Nyamia-Kpilo (great God); the Apolonians, Nana-Nyamale (Grandfather God, God-King); the Abure, Bedi-Nyamia (strong God); the Fanti, Ewladze-Nyako-pono (sole Master God).

"God is on high, behind the clouds, everywhere that one sees the sky. God is one, although he is a twin (Aflahui-Nyamia-Nda). God is also called 'he who attracts all the metals' (read 'powers') of the earth. No power equals his own.

If it seems hard to understand the economic, artistic, and social life of a people as well as their psychology without reference to the system of fundamental symbols that animates them, one cannot approach African culture without mentioning the special features of African spirituality. In African spirituality can be discerned man's attitude toward the sacred, his place in the scheme of creation, his feeling of belonging to the pan-structured universe.

In Africa, man is permeated with a world that is crowded, studded with a myriad of signifiers, visible and invisible, penetrating every facet of life. This world is dominated by the presence of a Supreme Being, a universal ruler presiding over the destinies of humans,

---

"Aflahui-Nyanome means he who makes the rainbow burst forth, who drives the impure from his throne. He is above any conspiracy.

"Nyamia-Kolafe means almighty God whom none can resist. God divides the occupations among men, for the good of all. And so it is that the healers care for the sick and the fishermen and farmers feed society. An herbalist who knowingly uses a bad substance, a fisherman who is jealous of his neighbor's luck, he who kills his fellow man, all sin against God's law, which forbids envy, theft, malice, adultery, and murder. Whoever is at peace with his soul is also at peace with God.

"God blesses the labor of the patient and curses that of the dishonest and the envious. He scolds evildoers with his thunder, and with his lightning he destroys wicked spirits. On him hangs the life of the genies as well as that of men.

"Except for those who take pleasure in impurity, all spirits worship God and present their offerings to him. Before caring for the sick, a genie always asks for his blessing, for there is no effective remedy outside of him. Through the mouths of their priests, the gods sing of their submission with gladness:

'I thank God,
It is God who produced me,
I thank God,
Okyondwe-e'" [p. 41].

animals, plants, things. Though this God (who is given a name in some areas; see Dika Akwa, 1971) is not specifically worshipped and there are no altars to him, though he is considered remote and inaccessible, he is nevertheless alluded to in many situations,[5] and it is possible, as Dika Akwa shows, to isolate a few characteristics (valid for the whole of Black Africa) regarding his origin, attributes, functions, modes of action, and influence.

Eternal and omniscient, God the creator is at the center of existence even though he has withdrawn from the world of humans, for he can make himself manifest on the earth, in the air, or in the water, at any time, in the most diverse forms. He is a hidden force, an imperceptible energy that diffuses throughout the whole expanse of the cosmos, determining the cycles of the seasons, the movements of the stars, the activities of the four great natural elements (rain, wind, vegetation, and lightning). In short, his power and dominion are boundless.

Ancestor of ancestors, God the creator is, in a certain sense, both immanent and transcendent.[6] The extra-

[5]Attribution of a theophoric name (a common practice in central and western Africa, where a newborn may be given such a name or an initiate rebaptized) provides evidence that God participates — indirectly — in life here below. See "Les noms théophores" in *Afrique et Parole* (1972).

[6]Thomas and Luneau (1975) speak of the "absent presence" of God: "God remains wrapped in paradox and that is really the only way he is. Without altar, without image, always elsewhere. And yet it is to him that people turn, in silence, with a simplicity of approach and of gifts offered, whenever the future of the community is gravely threatened. Any religious conception that tries to place man face to face with God without taking into account both phases of the process seems to us to truncate the reality of life and for that very reason, to make it partly unintelligible" (p. 142).

ordinary distance that separates God and men requires the intervention of relays or intermediaries (genies, spirits, ancestors);[7] communication must be established at all levels, so that ultimately the sacred permeates everyday life. According to Zahan (1970):

> The African may use all of the "materials" that his environment puts at his disposal in order to express his ideas about God. For him everything that surrounds him exhibits a sort of transparency that allows him to communicate, so to speak, directly with heaven. Things and beings are not an obstacle to the knowledge of God, rather they constitute signifiers and indices that reveal the divine being [p. 15].

God's withdrawal (which for the African explains the separation of earth and sky) leaves man great freedom of action.

Almost all African creation myths contain the theme of the sky originally lying flat against the earth. The contiguity of the two worlds was a great nuisance to human beings, sometimes impeding their growth or activities; women, especially, found it impossible to pound their grain without bumping awkwardly against the sky. This neighborly relationship was finally brought to an end by the wrath of the sky, which, vexed by the blows from the women's pestles, decided to move away from the earth.

[7]Among the men who have close relations with the divine are the priest (dealing with the sacred), the king (dealing with power), the griot (dealing with speech), the blacksmith (dealing with fire), and the diviner (dealing with the invisible).

A similar theme is just as frequently found concerning the relations between God and men. According to this theme, "God was once living among men (or men were living in the sky, close to God). Then, following incidents between the two parties, God resolved to recede from men" (Zahan, 1970, p. 16).

This withdrawal of God vis-à-vis his creatures (cf. Jaouen, n.d.), far from being felt by men to be the result of their erring ways (it is not a question of sin causing the sinner to fall from paradise to earth), marks instead a liberation willed by the creator (the same sort of liberation that is found in weaning from the mother's breast, a way of attaining a social status); it is up to men to turn their freedom to good account. In so far as men abide by a certain order fixed by creation and respect the hierarchical organization of worlds and of individuals, they have the power to build a universe to measure and to manage their own lives (cf. Kagame, 1968–1969).[8]

In Black Africa one of the best ways of getting to the heart of the relationship between man, God, and the world is, as we shall see, through mythology, because myths harbor the most primal symbols of the culture. The tales they relate express and interpret the order of the world; mythology also fixes the hierarchy of creatures and the precedence of tasks and activities within that world. The great cosmogonic theories of the Bambara, of the Dogon, of the Bantu are cultural conquests of a "natural" space that needs to be organized, ordered

[8]N.B.: The reader is referred to the many rich and well-documented articles concerning religion and spirituality in Black Africa that have been published in *Cahiers des Religions Africaines*, under the direction of the Faculty of Theology at Louvanium (Kinshasa) in Zaïre.

at every level, to avoid a return to the original chaos.[9]

Rituals, notably initiation rites, put mythology to the test, bringing it up to date; they make it possible to subject such a highly structured cosmos to periodic "remodeling."[10]

First and foremost, Africans want to understand the origins of the panstructuration of the universe. Myth, "a body of words, built up in tradition, with a view to providing an image of the underlying nature of things, of the organization of the universe" (Colin, 1965), establishes the necessary correspondence between social order and cosmic order, as well as revealing the mechanisms that are at the core of the operation of the uni-

---

[9]According to Thomas and Luneau (1975), myth "sanctifies the definitive triumph of life over death, of the pure over the impure, of order over disorder. Whether cosmological (concerning the structure of the world) or etiological (concerning origins), myth is always directly connected with the forces that determine the architecture of the world and the meaning of the universe, at the conjunction—through the medium of ritual—of the timeless and concrete time, a source of perpetually renewed emotion" (p. 148).

[10]Bambara myths (analyzed by Dieterlen, 1951) form an impressive metaphysical account, comprising a knowledge not only of the events of creation but of the principles of the state and course of those events:

1. creation is described as a continuous movement, going on forever, originating in a "vibration of both sound and light," and containing masculine power and feminine power (hence the androgyny of God the creator);

2. the universe rose out of the void, out of nothing (likened to chaos), forming a whirlwind imbued with a "humming" voice, that of Ngala (God);

3. space is organized into seven zones of sky, seven zones of earth, and seven zones of water; on earth, God presides over the events in the lives of human beings: birth, circumcision, excision, initiation, marriage, the cultivation of crops, travel, and warfare.

verse (from the etiological and functional points of view).[11]

Myths of origin therefore make it possible to put the basic elements (complementary or contradictory) back in place, and the ordering of these elements brings equilibrium to life — cosmic equilibrium, social equilibrium (lineage structures, relationships of affinity), and political equilibrium (sociopolitical systems).

As Zahan remarks (1970):

> It is interesting to note that these "creation" myths often go hand in hand with a certain social organization in the ethnic groups from which they stem. Among the peoples of northern Yatenga, for example, society is divided into two categories: the Foulse and the Nioniosse. To the first group is assigned the chieftaincy and it is always from among its members that the kings of Loroum are chosen, whereas the second group is concerned with the cult of the earth itself as well as with all the customs pertaining to its nourishing soil. Furthermore, according to their myths of origin, the Foulse came down from the sky while the Nioniosse rose up from the bowels of the earth. Far from merely expressing the actual pattern of social relations between groups, as one might naïvely think, these correspondences (which one encounters elsewhere in Africa) are rooted in the human subconscious.

[11]According to Holas (1964), "One of the principal purposes of myth, in its original, effective form, is to attune mankind to the rhythms of the cosmos, by teaching men ways to utilize the forces that the cosmos produces, by opening up for them the doors to the sacred, and by impressing on them an eternal cyclical movement according to a chronology that is not of this world" (p. 102).

There they arrange themselves around the concepts of order and harmony that are reflected by the social organization of all African peoples [p. 7].

Man needs his position to be defined within the complex of living beings. Mythology offers a picture of a three-tiered space, with constant interaction between the levels; the world is an architectonic structure in which each element is necessary to the whole, and a vast network of interconnections unites man with the universe, the living with the dead and with the spirits (Griaule, 1948).

The highest universe (the macrocosm) is the one where God resides and, close to him, the Ancestor, then the spirits of the chosen dead.

The intermediate universe (the mesocosm) is like a no-man's land, where chance reigns along with the disquieting strangeness of natural laws — a place of sojourn for wandering spirits, for genies, but also the scene of the nocturnal activities of *suntubon* (sorcerers). In fact, the special preserve of this mesocosm, a space of the individual and collective imaginary, begins at the edge of the village and hence encompasses, in large part, the bush and the forest, that is, natural, uncultivated space.[12]

[12]"There is many a madman who shouts and sings by the evening, though he left his village or dwelling in the morning perfectly sane. This is because he has passed under a tamarind tree at midday, and has seen there what he should not have seen: the inhabitants of another world, spirits which he had offended by his words or actions.

"Many a woman weeps and laughs, shouts and sings in the villages, driven out of her mind because she has poured boiling water from a cauldron on to the ground and scalded the spirits who were passing by or who were resting in the courtyard of her dwelling. These spirits have waited for her in the shade of a tamarind tree and made her lose her wits" (B. Diop, 1947, pp. 4–5).

The more limited universe of practical everyday life of man himself (in most cases, one could say the village) is the "socialized" microcosm.

Within each universe are multiple hierarchies. The mesocosmos is of special interest to us because it is the place, the milieu par excellence, where African culture locates overt or covert conflicts, all the more readily in that there is a similarity of structure and organization between mesocosmos and microcosmos: genies and spirits have their families, lineages, and age groups, just like humans — and the two realms are in constant interaction. This is one of the principal reasons for the continuity we have observed between African thinking about the imaginary (the structured collective imaginary) and African thinking about immediate social reality:

> Listen more often
> To Things rather than Beings.
> The Voice of the Fire can be heard,
> Hearken to the Voice of the Water.
> In the Wind
> Listen to the sobbing of the Bush:
> It is the Breath of the Ancestors.
> Those who have died have never departed:
> They are in the shadow that grows bright
> And in the shadow that thickens.
> The dead are not underground:
> They are in the tree that rustles,
> They are in the forest that moans,
> They are in water that flows,
> They are in water that sleeps,

They are in the hut, they are in the crowd —
The dead are not dead
                    ["Souffles," B. Diop, 1960, p. 64].

Since there is a structural identity between the microcosmos and the mesocosmos, with the two encompassed
by the macrocosmos, which has direct relations with
them, the universe should be thought of as being interwoven rather than layered — or as Paques (1954) has put
it, each element of the composite is an image of the
totality. Thus the whole appears to have a unity: the
cosmos is both hominized and humanized to a high
degree — that is, made by man and for man.

The traditional African knows that, at his own level,
he has a responsible part in the running of the world.
Myth invites him to "recreate" the world, that is, to
ceaselessly renew it, such renewal complementing, as it
were, the rhythm of the universe which is expressed in
the cycle of succeeding generations, in the alternation of
day and night and of the seasons as well.

Furthermore:

No one should be condemned to stay "in his place."
Man should work, should struggle to improve not
only his own life but, especially, that of others, that
of society. One must never — never, never — remain
in place: we have a duty to change the time that is
slipping by, the mountains that are watching us
with insolent eyes, the ground that is hiding from
us the treasures in its bosom, and, above all, men,
society. We must change all that, not only change
but also improve, bringing a breath of fresh air,
lighting up our life with the incandescent sun of a

new and radiant world. To stay in one's place, no, a thousand times no, for that is to close the door to happiness and progress [Matip, 1962, p. 365].

But myth also serves as a system of ethics, offering heroic models with which to identify; it outlines the stages by which the individual (in the beginning incomplete, unformed, and immature) attains the status of full human being through a series of initiations (see, *inter alia,* the remarkable text recorded by Ba and Dieterlen, 1961).

According to Senghor (1959), ethical conduct consists of living men and women recognizing the oneness of the world and working to achieve its unity. It is their duty, therefore, to improve their own lives but also to help realize the humanity of others.

The idea of order is at the heart of any religion, and religion shapes family, corporate, and state structures. Thus order is a prime concern of African society, deeply permeating the culture.[13]

The simple organization of living space (the arrangement of the dwelling and the village) often answers to precisely that concern for orderliness that is at the base of the relationship between the individual and his environment.

Similarly, we know that the architecture of certain buildings reflects the structure of the cosmos.[14] Some-

[13]"Civilization is an architecture of responses. Its perfection, like that of any dwelling house, is measured by the comfort man feels in it, by the added portion of liberty it procures for him" (Kane, 1961, p. 69).

[14]Although this structural homology is very striking among the Dogon of Mali as well as among the Fali and the Bamileke of Cameroon, it is commonly found everywhere.

times, just like humankind, the house serves to crystallize a complex symbolism; for example, being both male and female, it is appropriate for procreation. As Lebeuf (1961) notes, as "the locus of the life of the family, for whom it constitutes both the beginning point and the end point, the house forms a comprehensive picture of the life of the universe." Representing the smallest division of the cosmos, it is an infrastructure entirely subject to organization and control by human beings and, at the same time, a superstructure expressing, at the highest level, a conception of the universe.

A larger unit, the village, too, typically illustrates the concern for fitting social life into a framework structured along dynamic lines.

Natural space is also not a fixed and inert feature,[15] based on simple spatial coordinates, terrestrial and celestial. The structure of the universe, from its very foundation, is thought of in terms of opposite pairs (high-low, sky-earth, sun-moon), which evoke not only the alternation or complementarity necessary to the functioning of the system,[16] but also kinship terminology including the most complex symbolism (e.g., the sun-moon couple, which also expresses the opposition between the sun's stability and permanence and the moon's changeability and transformation). The cosmos, far from being cold and silent, is charged with symbolic

[15]For religious persons, the cosmos lives and speaks. Life is experienced on a twofold level: it unfolds as human existence and, at the same time, it shares in a transhuman life, the life of the cosmos or of the gods.

[16]Zahan (1970, p. 67) points out that space is usually organized and assessed in terms of its East-West axis: East = life, health, well-being, the direction one turns to seek the help of the divinity in day-to-day life; West = sickness, evil.

meanings. It contains within itself all the possibilities of the microcosmos, the social domain of man.[17]

Thus "the individual and the society to which he belongs constitute an uninterrupted chain of orderings leading from the visible link to the very borders of the universe" (Zahan, 1970, p. 80).

The same concern for order is found in the sphere of social organization, which is an extension of the organization of the physical world and is similarly determined by the need for continuity of the chain — peace, security, harmony.

To the African way of thinking, contemporary society represents a limited group of individuals (the living) within a vast community made up mostly of the dead, ancestors and other deceased. In regard to how society operates, the group of the living is organized on structural and hierarchical lines (the horizontal and vertical dimensions, respectively). One finds that a multitude of subgroups exist, with well-defined functions, forming veritable "social cells" that enable the community to maintain its power and increase its efficiency.[18]

---

[17]Not only does man envisage space, he "refashions" it. Just as he rebuilds a house after the death of an inhabitant, or a village after the death of a generation, man symbolically renews space at regular intervals (e.g., the Sigui ceremonies of the Dogon held every six years).

[18]Kouyate (1964) has described the situation in the following way: "For us. . . the group was the reality, the sovereign good, the refuge, the citadel without which the individual would be imperiled. Man moves about, evolves, fulfills himself within the group. Total rejection — rejection and rupture — is heresy. It leads to disintegration of the group, leaving the individual fragile, dooming him; it is suicide. . . . Why the group? Why this primacy? Because without it the individual could not, in good reason, exist. How would one face all those dangers that threatened, and today still

Among other things, therefore, initiatory associations facilitate the progressive integration of the individual into the group (their temporal aspect) as well as ensuring communication between the microcosmos, the mesocosmos, and the macrocosmos. Religious or fraternal societies (e.g., the Senufo Poro) assume responsibility for liturgical practices and maintain the tie between God and human beings; professional associations or "guilds" of hunters, fishermen, farmers, blacksmiths, weavers, etc. (e.g., the Mossi Singa) regulate the group's principal activities and ensure optimal conditions for carrying out vital economic tasks; political groupings (secret societies such as those of the panther men or leopard men in central Africa) defend the community against outside threats (sometimes taking the offensive, if necessary); associations of a moral or judicial order (e.g., the Nkutsu in the Congo) protect the community against internal threats, interpersonal conflict, and dissension; therapeutic groups, as we have seen, fill a dual role: prophylactic and curative.

The various institutions an individual must turn to, which he has to consult or participate in, are all means of human regulation in order to preserve the social order (which, as I have tried to show, has numerous interdependent coordinates linking it to the ancestors) at the level of the lineage, the village, and formerly the state. Some institutions play a more repressive role (with their

---

threaten, life in Africa? The brush fires that consume property, the animals that threaten the crops, the rains that come too little or not at all, ushering in famine, the huts that collapse, the diseases that cripple or kill . . . and so on. Only a solid, strongly structured group can be that citadel for the individual, guaranteeing his meager existence" (pp. 120–121).

methods of combating crime, disease, etc.), whereas others play a more preventive role (through prohibitions, rules governing alliance by marriage, blood pacts, etc.)

The adult conforms — the same as one conforms to ancestral law and obeys those who hold power — by virtue of the rule of primogeniture: succession of the generations and respect due to age (the general principle of seniority).

The traditional extended family, representing the basic unit of African society, assigns the individual a precise place (in relation to the family and to the group as a whole), a place that is kept and respected. Thus a person is defined in relation to the community he belongs to and in relation to his own lineage, in accordance with various parameters that determine a person's individuality: order of birth (firstborn or lastborn); sexual category; possible resemblance to a living relative or a forebear; status related to age class, to level of initiation, to caste at birth — with the conditions governing status depending on the kinship system followed by the ethnic group (matrilineal or patrilineal descent).

For example, among the Agni of the Ivory Coast (matrilineal), what is called the "affiliate" or clan is the result of a long history of splitting and scattering of the original seven tribes described in the creation myth. The present clans have no memory of those original groups, and each considers itself an autonomous community and has its own name (usually the name of the village where the subgroup first settled). The affiliate (or Appolonian *abusua*), the extended family of the mother, includes not only the direct descendants of a common ancestor (i.e., lineage or kin by uterine consanguinity) but also persons without status (without a recognized maternal uncle)[19] who have been incorporated into the ancestral descent group, or accepted for integration at their request. The clan is made up of branches descended from daughters and granddaughters of the common ancestor; each branch is headed by a "court queen," whose powers are delegated, however, to the "court chief" (the man representing force and authority, whereas the woman is the guarantor of right). The patriarch of the tribe and the court chiefs, on the one hand, and the queen of the tribe and the court queens, on the other, make up the "tribal council." It is this council that settles disputes and governs the material and spiritual life of the tribal members (Amon d'Aby, 1960, pp. 127–136).

Despite the institutions established to prevent it, disorder can erupt at any moment, in the form of physical calamities (natural catastrophes, such as flood or drought, and human catastrophes, such as disease, repeated failure in life, epidemic, sterility, death) or social calamities (war, dissension between individuals or groups). To combat disorder that arises, the community has numerous institutionalized systems of defense and arbitration at its disposal, making it possible to trace a theme and then formalize the existential trou-

---

[19]See I. Sow, 1977, chap. 5 ff. This is the case of the uterine nephew without a maternal uncle, or of a nephew "added" to the paternal lineage (a spurious lineage in matrilineal societies) or "taken back," in accordance with the marriage laws, in payment of some old kinship debt within the extended family.

bles of groups or individuals, particularly, by always trying—through a synthetic, structural diagnosis—to tie together the seemingly separate aspects of cultural, mental, and social life (individual and collective) into a comprehensive dynamic reality.

One major theme of traditional thought would seem to be the idea that anarchy carried to the extreme gives rise to a regeneration of the system as a whole, a principle underlying all the well-known techniques of dramatization, which are used at virtually every level of social activity to resolve and/or overcome conflict. For example, even the death of a parent, the end of a generation, can be experienced as an occasion of renewal for the living. Indeed, as Thomas and Luneau (1975) suggest, perhaps:

> we must admit that "rejuvenation by immersion in chaos" is a requirement for revitalization or regeneration that is characteristic of all societies (revolution and war, festivals, orgies, carnivals. . .) and particularly of archaic [read "traditional"] societies, perhaps because they have no other means of enduring through renewal, of confirming their values save by challenging them [p. 68].[20]

[20]In Black Africa and, in a more general way, in all consensual traditional societies, it is, of course, a matter of organized "chaos," conforming to a precise "order" whose parameters are controlled by skilled directors.

In any event, this is far from the simplistic creationist imagery that some writers have thought necessary to ascribe to traditional African societies, in particular, certain self-styled missionaries, professing to be Catholic, ingenuous in their dogmatism, more often stupid than malicious.

Most African ritual procedures[21] repeat in their basic
sequences that return to original chaos with a view to rebirth and recreation, to transcendence of present uncertainties. On the other hand, sometimes they mimic an
organized rebellion, a dramatized negation of the order
imposed by the powers that be in the daily life of the
community. But the ambivalence, whether it be latent
or expressed — the ambiguous feelings concerning the
dialectic complex of order and disorder (the foundation
of the present social order) — at times quite obviously
provides some understanding, in terms of periods of
greater or lesser internal tension and conflict, of the
possible conditions of the dynamic intragroup process.
Or put in another way, current cultural equilibrium is
the consequence and culmination of a series of prior
crises.

In short, a psychiatrist should always familiarize
himself with the structuring conditions and codes laid
down by the cultural frame of reference. Consequently,
with a view to developing a dynamic, comprehensive
approach and method, he should try to trace out at least
the principal systems and structures that go to make up
and mold an African from the anthropological point of
view.

The evolution of the African person/personality,
from birth to death, represents a continuous progression

[21]"Ritual enters into all human activities — fishing, hunting, farming, the
daily round as well as the high points of village life. Uniting the group,
sublimating social tensions, resolving conflicts, giving fresh impetus to the
community, controlling the risks of catastrophic weather, assuring the continuity of the clan phylum, reconciling earthly and divine powers — such
are the principal functions of ritual activity, of those 'cultural dramas' that
release pent-up energy" (Thomas and Luneau, 1975, pp. 203–204).

from the cosmic to the social, from nature to culture, from the external to the internal, from the formless to the formed, from the "empty" to the "full," from the nonrecognized to the recognized, from the meaningless to the meaningful, from nonbeing to being, and so on.

The child becomes a person in his own right; above all, however, he becomes a person for others and in relation to others. The main thrust of a child's education seems to me to be a sort of "hypopsychologization" combined with a "hyperculturalization" of individual outlooks and behaviors, which presume a whole enveloping framework and environment to be at work in the transmission of knowledge and know-how pertaining to the cultural order itself.[22]

Very briefly, to clarify my argument, I maintain that education in Africa should be viewed as proceeding along axes in three separate dimensions (see also Erny, 1972):

The biolineal dimension: integration of the child, then the adolescent into the clan phylum (establishing the child's position in relation to the ancestors accounts for the procedure of identification after birth; insertion into the lineage gives the child a special status in relation to the real father and to classificatory fathers in a patrilineal system, and in relation to the mother's brother and to classificatory maternal uncles in a matrilineal system);

---

[22]"Culturalization and socialization, on the one hand, and integration into the cosmos and the village, on the other hand, have but a single aim: to situate the child, to protect him, to help him fulfill his destiny within a group in orderly fashion, that is, in harmony" (Thomas and Luneau, 1975, p. 213).

The horizontal dimension: integration into circles of intense sociality — initiation societies, age-grade associations (or their functional equivalents) — enabling a person to develop throughout life, as he advances in age with his set, a whole solidarity-competition complex as well as a sense of community and, sometimes, to acquire the skills needed in adult professional life (in this connection, see the outstanding collection of articles on West African age classes and associations edited by Paulme, 1971);

The vertical dimension proper (i.e., religious): based on the ancestors, who lead to God; depending on the system, responsibility for this area of education falls to the mother's brother (matrilineal) or to the father (patrilineal).

These dimensions of African upbringing are what, on the one hand, ensure the continuation of tradition and, on the other hand, open the way to the knowledge and development necessary for the attainment of wisdom, an attribute of old age, when one has withdrawn from narrow political tribulations and becomes a heeded adviser.

In the words of Zahan (1970):

> It is the past that gives measure and volume to this completion, on the condition that man relies on the experience and wisdom of the generations that preceded him, that he agrees to be subject to the authority of the ancestors and tradition, and that he accepts their example as the stimulus and norm of his behavior. . . .

The African, living according to tradition, sees

progress above all as the realization by a given generation of stages that others have reached before it. It is always the present generation that is at the point of progress, but this generation is in some way unconscious of the acquisitions that it makes and that will form the first step for the next generation in its own climb to the past. Any religious or social innovation is thus less profitable to its authors than to those who come after them. Like the ideal, progress too is intimately linked to the past [p. 51].

In Africa, sexual union would be incomprehensible without its extension: procreation. Pregnancy is always the herald of imminent good fortune, which must be "cultivated in modesty and purity" (Amon d'Aby, 1960, p. 75), whereas sterility and miscarriage are considered calamities both for the parents and for the group.[23] A newborn child is, on the one hand, a guarantee for the future (a future worker) and a perpetuation of the group (he ensures continuity) and, on the other hand, a living symbol of the ties and continuity that exist between human beings, the spirits, the ancestors, and God. Hence the importance of birth and the conditions in which it takes place: it is not enough to be born, one must be well born,[24] which presumes proper preparation of the mother for childbirth and proper care for the newborn from the first moments of life.

[23]"Sterility is the negation of femininity and life. A sterile woman is vile and dead in life" (Memel Foté, 1962, p. 40).

[24]Furthermore, not only must one be born biologically (individual "uterine" birth), one must be born socially as well (rebirth of the group) — hence the importance of birth and rebirth sequences in initiation rites.

In procreation, the woman has the greater responsibility. Was she not the nest, indeed the in-
cubator of the progenitive egg? As mother, she is
incontestably the intermediary agent between the
"Supreme Force" and creation. As for the man,
once again, he is but a secondary contributor to the
multiplication of humankind. What is more
divine, what is greater or more beautiful than to
create?...Admit, my son, that woman has a role
of the first order, almost equal to the "Supreme
Force."...Because of the physiological complexity
of her whole being, the biological refinement of
her nature, woman is the "garden" of life. She is the
ornament of nature and the little sister of God,
whereas man is but his nephew [Malonga, 1954,
pp. 202–203].

Woman, the agent of life, is respected as a procreator. The various practices related to pregnancy
(preparatory rituals) are significant in that regard. The
mother-to-be is the object of many special attentions at
the various stages of the prenatal period (ablutions
aimed at preventing abortion, at avoiding disorders of
the blood or of the nervous system in the fetus). Moreover, she engages in certain symbolic practices that are
reputed to preserve or enhance fertility (caring for a
"fertility doll" or carrying a "fertility staff" for protection against witches, reciting chants, etc.). Above all
she is obliged to observe numerous prohibitions aimed
at avoiding any impurity: when an Agni woman is preg-
nant, she must wear white beads and immaculate
clothing, and should not be found wanting in either

fidelity or charity (especially in regard to old people, children, and the sick); she must also never wear mourning garb, participate in funeral rites, or go near animal carcasses; and she should be wary of strangers, spirits, and the ancestors.

The delivery itself is always accompanied by offerings, sacrifices, prayers, and invocations to the spirits and the ancestors. After the placenta has been buried (beneath the earth floor of the dwelling or in the courtyard),[25] the newborn is bathed and carefully examined, with a view to providing an initial identification (which may lead to bestowal of a first name) as well as to reassuring the group on the auspiciousness of the birth.

In the eighth month of pregnancy the expectant mother generally retires to her parents' home, where she remains confined until after delivery takes place. She neither comes out nor shows her baby until the day fixed by tradition or designated by the diviner for the official coming out and return to the village with the purpose of presentation and consecration of the newborn (integration rites).

This ceremony, which takes place a few days or weeks after birth, marks the child's entry and acceptance into the village community. Numerous prayers, sacrifices, and purification procedures to protect the newborn and those around him from the dangers that may assail them are preceded, accompanied, or followed, as the case may be, by a baptismal ceremony, which consists of an identification recognized by all, also governed by

---

[25]According to the well-known "rhythm," death and life are closely bound up with each other; to be born down here is to die in the beyond, and, conversely, to die down here is always to be born in the beyond.

precise rules. In almost all of West Africa, the customary ceremony of name giving takes place on the eighth day after birth and is accompanied by the ritual of placing the newborn on the mother's back.[26]

When the baby is thought to be the reincarnation of an ancestor, he or she is often given the name of a male or female forebear, especially if there is a physical resemblance. Children may also be given other names, in memory of a close friend or benefactor, or in commemoration of some event (war, rain, drought, etc.) that coincided with their coming into the world; they may have a name corresponding to their rank or day of birth, a social name, and a secret name (a surname peculiar to consanguineous relatives, which is used to designate a person only by mourners on the day of his death).[27]

The giving of a name, which constitutes the very essence of the individual as well as a link between the visible and the invisible, expresses the idea of reincarnation. Among the Agni, for example, when a name is given, all those present repeat the chant of welcome *"Akoa abao"* — "You departed and you have come back to life."[28]

[26]Naming sometimes takes place upon the appearance of the first teeth; it may be supplemented later by bestowal of a new name at initiation time, to mark the metamorphosis of the individual, to certify his new status (cf. Bernard, 1962, and Liénart, 1968).

[27]I have already mentioned the frequency of "theophoric" names (evoking some divine action). It should also be noted that until the day a child is formally given his real name, it usually remains a well-kept secret by the family.

[28]The multiplicity of names is matched by a multiplicity of identifications: in fact, a person finds himself offered several models on which to elaborate (so he has several openings onto reality, life, and personal development).

The rituals marking the beginning of life (severance of the umbilical cord, coming out, presentation-consecration, first placement on the mother's back), like the therapeutic procedures proper, provide for the integration of an individual characterized by inadequacy, incapable, on his own, of conforming to the requirements of community life that are of prime concern to the group: identification of everyone in terms of cultural parameters, respect for alliances, recognition of countless complex statuses and distinctions.

> Here I am again, you who used to speak to me through the brightness of the sky, through the song and flight of birds, through dreams, through the dawn and the dusk, tempests and hurricanes, through the zephyr and the breeze, plenty and dearth, I turn to you to give new structure to society, fresh vigor to young shoots and old limbs. . . .
>
> I come back to you for my equilibrium and for peace in the country, peace among all those who dwell together, peace between those of the forest and ourselves, peace between those of the water and ourselves, peace between those of the air and ourselves [Dadié, 1970, p. 133].

Child-rearing practices and attitudes follow the same general principles in widely separated regions of Black Africa. Here, there, and everywhere, one finds the same characteristic educational stages marking the social development of children. Numerous well-known clinical studies have been made, but have not yet been synthesized. Nevertheless, it seems to me that the divisions put forward by Zempleni-Rabain (1974) with respect to the Wolof child can serve as an illustrative framework.[29] For our purposes here, it is sufficient to review the outline:

The first period (from birth to about two years of age) is marked by close physical proximity to the mother (corresponding to the nursing and carrying phase); ushered in by the naming ceremony and placement of the newborn on the mother's back, encompassing the learning of speech and cleanliness, this period comes to a close with weaning, which is manifested in concrete terms by termination of the close body-to-body contact between mother and nursing infant.

The second period (from about two to five years of age) is the real beginning of social integration properly speaking; the child gains his first social knowledge and experience, which goes hand in hand with the development of physical play and verbal exchange with those around him. This phase is characterized by a process of decentering with respect to the exclusive figure of the mother; however, one always finds the continuing presence of substitute figures on a smaller scale, which lessens the magnitude of the possible separation trauma.

The third period (from five years of age to adolescence) is an extension of the preceding period,

[29]Another possible schema of development: (a) the first period: until cutting of the milk teeth (a period that is properly, but not exclusively, "maternal"; nursing and carrying, with the mother's back being the functional counterpart); (b) the second period: from cutting of the milk teeth to cutting of the permanent teeth (the lineal family, age groups; the beginning of intensive socialization proper); (c) the third period: from cutting of the permanent teeth to sexual maturity (marriage, procreation); initiation (where it occurs) and assumption of a sociopolitical role within the community; then, withdrawal from current affairs and assumption of the role of adviser (elder).

completing horizontal integration into the peer group, with the system of peers, of age classes and associations, ensuring eventual accession to the adult stage.[30]

The first period of development of the child's personality takes place in an especially permissive atmosphere, extending the state of symbiosis that precedes it. Numerous pediatricians have remarked on this fact, and those at Fann (Dakar) have called particular attention to it.

According to some pediatricians, however, the prolonged and intense character of this first relationship accounts for a number of clinical findings associated with weaning, such as loss of weight and slowed psychomotor development, which prior to weaning is notably fast in Africa compared to the average rate of development for children in other parts of the world.[31]

---

[30]In most African societies, the system of age classes (as it used to operate, very strictly) is undergoing complete transformation, but the same functions can be found in groupings structured along age lines as well as in the celebrated fellowship among schoolmates of the same class. Notwithstanding, the old initiation practices themselves still persist in basic outline, and some governments are currently reviving them, sometimes simplifying the ritual stages and/or shortening the duration of the trials. Be that as it may, everywhere, with no known exception, the rules of precedence, of respect due to difference in age, are completely intact even among the young university students of today, as can be readily verified in the field.

[31]One can contrast the Western system of child rearing, in which experiences of gratification and frustration alternate in time right from the start, with the African system, in which gratification and frustration are introduced successively in time, one following the other. In another respect, however, we know that in the African view, all development, all progress, all creation, is actually the result of some crisis, just as contemporary culture is itself the result of a series of earlier sudden and violent crises. In the case in question, the crisis involves modification of the mother-child bond, and experience shows that the early form of socialization that replaces it is completely satisfactory in construction of the personality.

African pediatricians tend to see those symptoms as merely transitory, which they are as a matter of fact. They can be considered "critical" symptoms, indirectly opening the way to a higher phase of development. Thus, in many respects, weaning calls to mind a difficult transition comparable to an initiation stage. In any event, as long as things are kept in check, "weaning symptoms" are simply the nursling's initial response to the first rupture of the bond. In a sense, then, they are a form of personal identification and the beginning of interchange with others.

The mother who used to relieve all tension arising in her baby by immediately satisfying his needs (offering him the ever-available breast, symbol of nourishment and passive security) suddenly calls into question this prototype relationship, which has to be abandoned. At the same time, moreover, she resumes sexual relations with her husband after a long period of abstinence. It should be understood that the mother-child pair as well as the parental pair, both in their makeup and in their functions, follow quite different patterns from those that are commonly found in an anthropological framework in which particular value is attached to individualistic relationships. What occurs is a veritable restructuring of the relational universe (cf. Collomb, 1965a, pp. 29 ff., and Zempleni-Rabain, 1966), not to the advantage of the narcissism of the parental couple alone (or of the reduced household in which the child is only a kind of fantasized appendage), but, and in my view this is fundamental, the process is beneficial to the child himself, seen in his own right as a highly social being.

As Zempleni-Rabain so perceptively points out, weaning is a negative but necessary experience to achieve the social integration of the child. The child was locked in a two-way relationship in which the components of nature and nourishment were dominant; with weaning he is introduced into the larger group, the conveyor of culture, dominated by social exigencies, in which the father and his substitutes will take on increasing importance.

Forming the basic cell of society as well as the socioeconomic unit of production, the extended family group is both the framework in which learning takes place and the reference system for apprehending the world in its different dimensions: microcosm, mesocosm, and macrocosm.[32]

As Kouyate (1964) points out:

> In Africa, someone who places himself outside the community, in one way or another, loses his quality of human being and becomes a kind of reincarnation of evil spirits, shunned and feared by all. . . . Man is born, grows, develops, and fulfills himself only within an encompassing whole which en-

---

[32]In fact, with respect to membership in the family group as a whole, the social expression of individual feelings prevails over all other forms of attachment; thus relationships between individual persons, which are highly formalized, are meaningful at a deeper level only in relation to cultural patterns.

All of which is to say that feelings (attraction, love, hate, etc.) are in fact, despite appearances, institutionalized in terms of their individual expression, and very markedly so, as in all traditional societies. Some modern metapsychologists think, a trifle naïvely, that love characterized by fusion, absolute and instinctive love (maternal love, for example), is a first, irreducible fact of so-called human nature, along with other platitudes of that ilk. Similarly, in the case of adult couples, people love each other according to a cultural pattern, even though they may not know it.

riches him and which he should enrich in turn. Outside of this idea, outside of this logic, there is no man [pp. 221–222].

The most immediate relationship in which the child is caught up is, of course, the one that, with the help and affection of the mother and father, binds him to the living biolineage — then, in a more indirect way, to the vertical dimension (to the forebears). It is this verticality that assigns him an ontological seat in the phylum, within a structured universe. This same vertical integration is recounted in vivid fashion by those genealogical troubadors, the griots. This line, which goes back to the principle of all life and which is simultaneously a phylogenetic, ontological, biological, and social reality, expresses the necessary association between the living and the dead, the ancestors close to God, forming a coherent system of deep relational networks. One always finds in Africa the latent presence of the primary symbolism of this "bond." The individual need not think of himself as an isolated atom; he is dependent though completely autonomous, being responsible for and bound up with others. Therefore, no relationship has any meaning except within a system of more fundamental ties to near kin and others (cf. Buakasa, 1972).

If the child has been suddenly separated from his mother, it is because he must become aware of others and their existence, instead of continuing to satisfy his own narcissism in a closed relationship. Human life is a series of dramas, one after the other, and Africans like to dramatize situations to help resolve them. This pedagogic principle explains the frequent and widespread custom whereby children are taken in and educated by relatives who often live far away (grandparents, aunts, uncles, but also friends or classmates of the parents, etc.). The same is true of the "circulation" of children of brothers (or sisters), which is practically the rule in all of Black Africa. Similar interpretation also accounts for what could be called the scaling down, very early, of mother figures. And, as we know, the social universe of the African infant, and later on of the African child, is essentially a mobile universe right from the start, alive and filled with speech, and not a world of untalkative objects.

As Kenyatta (1938) points out:

> The key to this culture is the tribal system, and the bases of the tribal system are the family group and the age-grades, which between them shape the character and determine the outlook of every man, woman, and child in Gikuyu society. . . . Nobody is an isolated individual. Or rather, his uniqueness is a secondary fact about him: first and foremost he is several people's relative and several people's contemporary. His life is founded on this fact spiritually and economically, just as much as biologically; the work he does every day is determined by it, and it is the basis of his sense of moral responsibility and social obligation. . . . [Tradition] shows how indispensably kinship is at the root of Gikuyu ideas of good and evil. This vital reality of the family group is an important thing for Europeans to bear in mind, since it underlies the whole social and economic organization [pp. 309–310].

In the same vein, Zempleni-Rabain (1974) reports:

> Almost all exchanges take place within a group situation. Face-to-face exchanges are carried on naturally and comfortably only if they are patterned on publicly sanctioned exchanges. Adults, leisurely engaged in routine activities such as peeling fruit or shelling peanuts, nursing the baby or playing with him as he climbs on the mother, are gathered together for hours at a time, while the conversation rambles idly or grows lively with joking retorts. Children of all ages are welcome to find a place in the circle, with the youngest having the broadest privileges of movement and contact. If the rhythm of activity of a three-year-old involves exploratory wandering to and fro, alternating coming and going, the presence of adults and elders, who are extremely accessible in this privileged realm of bodily proximity, is an invitation to contact, to physical and motor play [p. 31].

In the traditional pattern of upbringing, the child then enters the society of his peers (as early as five or six years of age in some cultural areas). The traditional organization into age classes or associations (cf. Paulme, 1971) provides training in community life, and hence preparation for adult activities that would be impossible outside of groupings, societies, or corporate bodies.[33]

From the social point of view, the system of age

---

[33]"Negro-African society is essentially an initiatory society of age classes, successive by training and integrating of the generations, one after the other" (Ki-Zerbo, 1972).

classes leads to microsocieties, which, though reg-
ulated, are relatively autonomous, having their own
traditions and operating on the principle of mutual education. Thanks to these microsocieties, the fundamental
mechanisms of identification are established, with the
"big brothers" of preceding classes serving both as
models and as the key to integration into the general
society, which is based on the principle of seniority, at
the core of which is the law of the ancestors. Thus even
today, everywhere, people continue to call each other
"my comrade," "my little brother," "my big brother,"
"my father so-and-so," etc., it being understood that
such a designation requires the corresponding type of
behavior and communication that convention calls for,
although quite obviously there is no bond of biological
kinship between the partners. From the psychological
point of view, this system encourages a general spirit of
equality, brotherhood, and attachment, of mutual help
and trust within the age group, but it also fosters, simultaneously, an intense, even implacable, competi-
tiveness in certain specific social situations.

All these features are vital to collective life — shared
work and play, under supervision by the next older children — and also help to create bonds of fellowship that
last throughout life. For example, when a person becomes an adult, he maintains very close relations with
his age mates, who are looked on as his real brothers not
only by him, but by the family and the entire community as well. In practical terms, in the village the age-class
system finds material expression in the designation of
certain tasks as the special province of children of a
given age, for instance, herding and watching the sheep

and goats for boys, gathering fruit and collecting dead-wood for the girls (Paulme, 1971).

Similarly, in some cases play areas are set up away from the village and family compounds. Also, separate living quarters may be established and built, specially arranged by and for children; thus boys may be grouped in a common hut (cf. Lapassade, 1963).[34]

Kenyatta (1938) provides an excellent description:

> The Gikuyu child does not need Montessori exer-cises or class-room lessons in manual dexterity, for with plenty of space to tumble about in, and with older people about him doing interesting manual jobs, he will naturally learn by real experiments. There is work for him to do as soon as he has ac-quired the skill to do it properly, and he hardly dis-tinguishes work from play. As he grows older the age-group gives him the democratic companion-ship of equals, and he learns by competition with other children the keenness of sense and agility of limb which will equip him for his life, as well as skill in the various operations of agricultural and pastoral work. He learns these things by imitation and free exercise, and to some extent at his own risk, and in doing so he learns how to behave to his seniors and how to get along with comrades of his own age. And since there is plenty of necessary ac-tivity, of a kind suited for every age, the steps of his

[34]The intensive socialization within the age class in effect implies a strict separation between children and parents, and paves the way for true "ac-culturation" of the child with initiation. The initiation process generally in-cludes three major phases, separated in space and time: separation (death), reclusion (marginality), reintegration (rebirth).

education are not just exercises for his own improvement, but real contributions to the needs of
the group life [pp. 312–313].

At a certain age, which may vary with the locality
though the principle remains the same, the passage of
the "watershed" age class to the status of initiates at the
next higher level is marked by initiation rites proper
(whereas the passage of an ordinary age class to the next
level is marked only by simple rites of passage). If
African initiation is traditionally experienced as a difficult, "critical" transformation, as a grievous and painful ordeal, physically as well as mentally,[35] the fact is
that in Black Africa, as I noted earlier, human existence
and life are thought of as punctuated by an intermittent
series of crises.

The problem that is posed is: How does one become
an adult? Can a person truly become adult through little "minicrises" (attenuated, moreover, by modern
parental anxieties)? Or must one prepare a crisis, pro-
voke it, supervise it, and thereby help to resolve it? That
is the problem, it seems to me, of any society: Is the passage to adulthood and the course through various ages
seen as a path of continuous progress (without interruption or break) or as a series of ordered and critical
ruptures going on until old age and death?[36]

[35]Its harshness, along with the painful experience of personal loneliness
during the initiation proper, revives and extends the crisis of weaning. The
trials aimed at transforming the child (nature) into a man (culture) were
formerly, at least, terribly severe. Some candidates could not stick it out. In
this connection, see especially Gaisseau's (1953) full and detailed account of
the initiation trials of the Toma (of the Guinea forest on the Liberian fron-
tier).

[36]According to Erny (1972), "growth is a series of passages through suc-

In any case, in traditional Africa, a full awareness of the formative value of such sudden ruptures for the purposes of self-renewal helps the neophyte to bear the trials and tribulations of initiation (seclusion, fasting, deprivation of sleep, nakedness, blows and wounds, burns, mutilation, aggravated fears, etc.), in short, all the most painful and frightening experiences that a man may have to go through in the course of his real life. In these terms, Laye (1953) recalls his own experience of the initiation ritual (at 14 years of age), showing that it is lived through as a consecration, which helps in mastering fear:

> We were lined up, each of us in front of a stone. At the other end of the clearing the men stood facing us. And we took off our clothes.
>
> I was afraid, terribly afraid, and I needed all my will power not to show it. All those men standing in front of us and watching us must see nothing of my fear. My companions showed themselves as brave as I, and it was absolutely necessary that it should be so. Perhaps a future father-in-law or a future relative was among those men standing in front of us. We dared not let ourselves down now!
>
> Suddenly the operator appeared. We had caught a glimpse of him the night before, when he had performed his dance in the main square. And now too I only caught a brief glimpse of him. I had hardly realized he was there before I saw him

---

cessive circles that partially overlap one another and go on expanding; each passage corresponds to a change of state, a step toward social maturity, bringing increased duties and responsibilities."

standing in front of me.

Was I afraid? I mean, was I even more afraid, had I at that particular moment a fresh access of fear — for I had been beset by fears ever since I had entered the clearing? I did not have time to be afraid. I felt something like a burn and I closed my eyes for the fraction of a second. I do not think I cried out. No, I can not have cried out. I certainly did not have time to do that either. When I opened my eyes the operator was bent over my neighbor. In a few seconds that year's dozen or so boys had become men. The operator made me pass from one state to the other with an indescribable rapidity [pp. 123–124].

Convinced of the necessity of suffering, of the social importance of courage and obedience, which determine promotion to adult status, the child manages to maintain remarkable mastery over himself.[37]

In initiation the drama of life is played out in strong terms, interweaving the individual and the social, the sacred and the profane, the real and the imaginary. Initiation represents not only a passage in time (transition from a lower or unfinished state to a higher or finished state) but also a crossing of space. For example, consider the initiation of a young Bantu girl of southeast Africa:

First state (Khomba): rules of the body, of the hearth and home;

Second stage (Tshikanda): domestic life, household rules

---

[37]Note the importance of body techniques in training for adult life; at the level of the body schema, dances imprint a sense of solidarity and foster self-control.

Third state (Domba): preparation for marriage and for family and social life, rules of the compound, discovery of the realm of the sacred, the meeting of the cosmic and the social (on the topological level: from the village to the bush; on the symbolic level: from culture to nature; on the metaphysical level: from the visible to creative energy). The individual approaches the macrocosm, but learns the secrets of the mesocosm (cf. Ngoma, 1963).

According to Cazeneuve (1971):

> At the same time that the adolescent leaves childhood to become a man, he comes into contact with the divine symbols of the human condition. . . . The act of assuming the human condition is not separable from sanctification of that condition. . . . If the neophyte leaves the world of his childhood, it is above all the world of the profane, the world of the uninitiated that he leaves behind. To mark a sharp division between the sanctified human condition and the uninitiated, the initiation ritual often takes on an aura of mystery for the uninitiated, who are kept away [pp. 268–269].

If the diversity of initiation rites (in terms of duration, location, essentially masculine or feminine character, techniques employed, applications)[38] and their hermetic aspect are disconcerting to the foreign observer, for our

[38]*Duration:* initiation may span a person's entire lifetime; among the pastoral Peul, for example, instruction (following the initiation text, *Koumen)* takes place in three sequences of 20 years each. *Location:* natural sites (bush, forest) are important, as are enclosures evocative of the fetal state (grottoes) and also secrecy (secret places and secret languages). *Divi-*

part, we are compelled to recognize in initiation phenomena a dramatic technique for training responsible sociocultural "cadres." To state it briefly, for the group, initiation is a way of training competent human beings who have mastered the essentials for dealing with life's problems; for the individual it provides self-assurance as, uprooted from a bygone past in psychodramatic fashion and without niceties, he enters a new category of full human being, ready to assume his social responsibilities. A general surge of vitality is felt on the occasion of the festivities, which give rise to the most diverse forms of expression, both at the individual level (body cathexis, erotic release) and at the community level (confrontations, games, exchanges, distribution of goods) (Zahan, 1960).

Taking into account both these dimensions of initiation, the individual and the group dimension, Thomas and Luneau (1975) stress the following aspects of initiation as well:

> Looked at sociologically, initiation seems to be a total social experience (in the sense of M. Mauss): the political, the economic, the cultural, the ludic — all closely interwoven — are combined with the

---

sion of the sexes: there is female as well as male initiation (although women "carry knowledge within them"); thus there are numerous rituals related to the first menstruation (cf. the puberty rites of young Venda and Bemba girls); also, the sexes may be brought together at adolescence (combined initiation). *Techniques employed:* numerous modes of expression include physical techniques (painful ordeals) as well as hypnagogic techniques (hallucinatory procedures, nakedness, sacrificial atmosphere, etc.). *Applications:* there are specialized groupings, with initiations preparing candidates for particular functions (warriors, diviners, healers, priests, blacksmiths, etc.).

sacred. *Existentially*, it is both an individual and collective drama through which the group transcends the trauma of the changes brought about by integration into the passage of time, and fixes the ranks and roles of its various members. . . . *Intellectually*, it emerges as a play of symbols based on the archetypal truths of myth and legend. . . . Lastly, *metaphysically*, it becomes a privileged dimension of the sacred, which, in its highest forms, can promote union with God, the supreme expression of ontological unity [p. 214].

Zahan (1960) has shown that the Bambara initiation societies (or *dyow*), which together "cooperate in the work of liberating and revitalizing man," concentrate, one after the other, on the discovery of some fragment of knowledge relating to man and his destiny. Representing the various stages in that knowledge, the *dyow* are six in number, and the Bambara call them by the following names: *n'domo, komo, nama, kono, tyiwara,* and *korè*. The order of this list is the same as that of the successive initiations every individual must go through to achieve enlightenment. These six societies are symbolically paired by the Bambara with the six major joints of the human body:

1. The *n'domo* (corresponding to the ankle) opens the road to knowledge, initiating the movement toward beings and things.

2. The *komo* (corresponding to the knee) deals with the nature of knowing and man's relations with knowledge.

3. The *nama* (corresponding to the hip joint) moves

on to procreation, to fecundity (creation of the family, preservation of the community).

4. The *kono* (corresponding to the elbow) promotes the union of body and mind.

5. The *tyiwara* (corresponding to the shoulder joint) teaches manual activities, notably agriculture.

6. The *korè* (corresponding to the wrist) is the highest path to spirituality.

> The extensive spiritual training of a Bambara consists of his initiation to the six *dyow*. Only that permits explicit revelation of the integral universe-man, which every initiate must realize in his soul and in his flesh [Zahan, 1960, p. 35].

Giving man the means to realize himself, providing the tools for his fulfillment, facilitating action, the initiation societies help to mobilize a person's motor system and sense organs, which put him in touch with his environment. Moving, touching, smelling, tasting, hearing, and seeing are the activities successively and selectively brought into play by the six Bambara *dyow*.

Viewed through the process of initiation, gaining experience of self would appear to be familiarization with the sacred, sexuality, and death.

Intended to familiarize the human being with the meanings of the world around him, initiation serves to complete the self through revelation of the most profound symbols, the foundation of all that is sacred. To the extent that it puts man in touch with the transcendent (by revealing symbols), initiation "sanctifies" man, sometimes carrying him to the highest degree of spirituality — contact and dialogue with the Divinity (the case of the Bambara *korè*). Very often, the initiate temporarily takes on a spiritual nature (withdrawal from humankind, retreat), then, endowed with this "capital," rejoins other humans.[39] The search for the invisible shows that man transcends himself also by plumbing his own depths.

Intended to familiarize the human being with the meanings of his own body (a privileged manifestation of life and its renewal), initiation also serves to complete sexuality. If the male and female states are precisely spelled out when procreation becomes feasible for boys and girls (often at the end of their initiation), the fact remains that, from their earliest years, children are prepared to assume their sexual role, that is, their function of procreator, in the service of the group.

Circumcision and excision (which often constitute the first step of initiation) have as their aim, it should be recalled (according to the traditional mythic account of the Dogon and Bambara, for example), the elimination of original androgyny: deprived of the foreskin, the boy becomes wholly "masculine"; deprived of the tip of the clitoris, the girl becomes wholly "feminine." These operations (regarded as veritable metamorphoses) would be devoid of interest were it not that they lead directly to an apprenticeship in sexuality.

In concrete terms, in a number of societies girls are prepared for the expression of genital sexuality through massage (or by elongation of the labia, as among the

[39]Holas (1956) has described the *Poro* initiation, which among the Senufo takes place in three phases, each stretching over seven years. The last phase (maturity, fullness of the initiate) includes return into the womb of the god Katieleo and rebirth (the moral being made divine and delivered anew).

Hottentots, for example), then trained through dancing to make hip movements that mimic sexual intercourse, and so on. Actually, sexual freedom is known to be very great almost everywhere, mainly before marriage between adolescents in central Africa, and only after marriage in west Africa, at least traditionally.

Among the peoples of southwest Africa, there is a period of communal life (combined initiation) called *oi-juuo*, when

> boys and girls are brought together and "play" at being married couples. They sleep together at night, and during the day perform tasks according to their sex, in imitation of the chores of married people. Boys pretend to be taking care of the cattle and go out to hunt small animals while their "wives" busy themselves in the kitchen preparing meals for their "husbands" [Zahan, 1970, p. 57].

Before marriage young people are always instructed in the duties that come with this new state. Since marriage involves the alliance of two families in the social and economic spheres (fundamental bonds of community life), wisdom, intelligence, and fairness should be exercised in managing the interests of the family group so as to contribute to the good of the community. In central and southern Africa, moreover, adultery is viewed as "theft" and treated accordingly.

Intended similarly to familiarize the human being with the meaning of change (passage from one state to another, from one status to another), relating mythic time to concrete time (present historical time), that is, connecting symbols with existence, initiation is also a

long preparation for death, bringing the living closer to
the deceased ancestors.

As we have seen, on the one hand, all initiation rites
include symbolic death and rebirth ("death of the old
man and resurrection of a new being"); on the other
hand, actual physical death, considered a "passage" (to
another life), is the occasion for rituals reminiscent of
initiation (trials to achieve the state of ancestor).

Death is not total destruction. Though the body, consisting of perishable matter, may be doomed to decom-
position, the imperishable, immaterial elements ensure
survival in the beyond. It is this survival that accounts
for the importance and complexity of the funerary rites,
aimed at preventing the soul from wandering (it is a
matter of integrating it with the other spirits of the
departed), at protecting the family from sorrow, and at
resealing the bonds between the living and the dead, in
a single everlasting communion.

Accession to the status of ancestor is a consecration;
there is nothing automatic about it, and it is graduated
just like initiation. Since founding Ancestors and mythic
Ancestors are near the seat of the divine creator, they
are never reincarnated. It is they who govern the living
in the sense that, as a body, they inspire, with all the
respect that is due them, the conscience and memory of
the group.

In such an all-encompassing anthropological perspective, sickness is, even more patently than elsewhere,
inextricably bound up with the cultural context. Saying
that, one can look at it from two points of view, synchronic and diachronic.[40]

_____

[40]"Above all, sickness has a meaning that cannot be understood outside

As I am attempting to show, if mental illness should always be viewed in terms of its principal dimensions, the most serious manifestations are invariably those that point to the latent relational conflict as being situated at the diachronic level and psychotic in character, whereas manifestations experienced in a synchronic mode usually express conflicts of a neurotic type (see I. Sow, 1977, chaps. 2, 3, and 8).

The father image (progenitive father, social father) is, in fact, the image of seniority as a whole, which by degrees merges into that of the community of ancestors. In no case could the father be a practical rival. This does not prevent there being, at least potentially, a generational conflict (diachrony); but such conflicts of a diachronic order, manifest or latent, are rooted exclusively in the desire to take over total political power in order to strengthen new cultural bonds. Clearly, the young African Oedipus — if one looks to his structure and the true nature of his symbolism — cannot be an incestuous, libidinous Oedipus, motivated by narcissism and individualism. The young African Oedipus is political or he is nothing at all.

---

the religious and cultural context peculiar to the ethnic group in question. That is why, whether it be a question of diagnosis or of treatment, only the bringing into play of a chain of signifiers that the sick person and the group to which he belongs hold to, without reservation, can prove effective" (Thomas and Luneau, 1975, p. 239).

CHAPTER FOUR

The Primordial Symbols
of African Anthropology
in Relation to
the Dynamics of Personality

Doctors have the task of reestablishing the con‐
tinuity of existence for subjects whose perspective
of life has been shattered. For millenia, such con‐
tinuity has been magically reestablished through
the socialization of concrete consequences of ill‐
ness; medical ideology is therefore utilization of a
society's myth systems. At the same time, it is an

essential factor in the development of a society's myths — every ethnologist is led to take medical myths into consideration within the meaning system of the society he is studying, for they are precisely the myths of human existence in the society in question [G. Daumezon, preface to Hochmann's *Pour une psychiatrie communitaire* (Paris: Editions du Seuil, 1971)].

I should like initially to point out to the reader that the discussion that follows does not proceed from analyses developed according to the structuralist method. Indeed, I am not a mythologist, and my much more modest aim is directed solely at trying to discover, in the myths and themes we shall touch on here, certain elements useful to our purpose, which remains, in a more central way, psychological and psychopathological inquiry. Our task will be to trace, all the way back to mythic creation (the collective imaginary), certain manifest and constant themes of daily life in Africa, such as persecution, aggressiveness on the part of outsiders, and, more generally, the relationship of violence to social practice and, ultimately, to the development of mental illness and its interpretation.

In my view, violence would seem to be at the origin and foundation of society and culture; it is from that point of departure, long ago, that the present consensus came to be established and then organized on the basis of contemporary distinctions, classifications, and hierarchies — in short, all order, at the end of which is the sacred Ancestor. The liturgy of today, conforming to prescribed and precise ritual sequences, commemorates

the deeds and expresses the Word of the Ancestor as related in the myths. Falling within the same symbolic
framework is the celebration of sacrifice in memory of
the primordial sacrificial victim that in far-off times became the focal point of intracommunity violence, thus
making it possible to establish the peace and order of
today.

It seems essential, then, even from our psychological
and psychopathological perspective, to draw attention
to the role of the sacred in African thought and culture,
for that underlying idea is what ultimately enables us to
understand the deep-seated connections between certain traditional themes and the perception of madness
as a relational conflict (aggression), recalling the primordial, chaotic times prior to civilization, characterized by confusion, violence, undifferentiation — in
short, perpetual insecurity with respect to individual
and social identity.

In the traditional African world, man possesses, one
could say, a sense of transcendence; beings and things
enjoy full reality only in so far as they have — or have
ascribed to them in the hierarchical scale of representations — an assigned place and name in a well-ordered
universe. In the final analysis, this means that, for the
African himself, genuine existence really begins only
after the symbolism has been grasped that connects existence, link by link, to the act of primordial genesis,
which brings fullness of meaning. Order, individual
and social peace, always signifies that one is at peace
with the ancestors, in order and hence right with them.
Madness means "rupture" and disorder; in that sense
disorder is desecration of the sacred. Thus it would be

vain to try to approach the idea of madness without reference to the origins, the sacred origins, of the system of representation of the universe and man's present existence, or in other words, without reference to the primordial symbols.[1]

According to the custodians of traditional learning, the symbols contained in myths form the corpus of authentic knowledge of a sacred nature, which is not revealed except under special ritual conditions; thus mythic symbols have the role of conveying the meaning of man's life and recalling the collective vicissitudes and sacrifices that form the basis and foundation of the present communal order. More often, however, that story in its complete and original form seems to have slipped from man's memory; sometimes even, nothing seems to remain but the ritual—or just fragments of ritual sequences—to commemorate the fundamental act of creation.

In the eyes of tradition—in Africa as elsewhere—mythology represents a patrimony charged with primordial symbolic meanings, which give it its importance. In addition to its more verifiable values, mythology serves as a paradigmatic axis around which are organized cultural life and the richest expressions of contemporary society. Thus one of its crucial functions is to restore meaning to rituals and, more generally, to provide a foundation for the principal meaningful activities of man. People of today are affected by the events that form the themes of mythic productions, because those

[1]"To try to understand Africa and Africans without the contribution of the traditional religions would be like opening a gigantic chest emptied of its most precious contents" (Ba, 1965, p. 8).

events changed the life and existence of men of that day in important and significant ways, and present-day men are their descendants and cultural heirs.

But before we can gain a full understanding of the symbols and foundations of African culture, several generations of African researchers will have to work at analyzing the oral material and thoroughly examining traditional themes. I remain convinced that there is a rich trove to be explored and exploited by intellectual circles; it will be the source that will feed the principal forms of cultural expression — theater, literature, all manner of artistic production.

Having said that, I repeat that my aim is infinitely more modest: taking as a point of departure mental illness and the problem raised by the violence inherent in the very concept of the sufferer as victim, so common in Black Africa, we shall follow the thread of the theme of persecution and the violent double in an effort to go back, through traditional themes, to the cultural sources (mythic symbols) of violence and so gain a better understanding of the meanings of persecution-aggression in mental illness.

Among possible approaches, two alternatives are open to us for examination of the myths:[2]

1. Either treat them as a fund of objective information to be subjected to mathematical analysis, a matter of purely formal architectonics; or

[2]It is out of the question, within the framework of the present study, to undertake a systematic and exhaustive analysis of all the themes conveyed in the myths mentioned here. Such a labor, a necessary one in my opinion, would have to be the focus of numerous studies; the common foundation developed in that way would form one of the "reservoirs" of African culture.

2. Look at them as an expression of the conscious, which is trying to convey, in the form of images and symbols, the essence of a particular anthropological experience — in short, as one of the dramatic modalities of the collective conscious. Seen in this second perspective, as the deployment of symbols, mythology constitutes the most basic level of social and cultural experience.

Inasmuch as my own contribution lies mainly in the sphere of interpretation and comprehension of the pathetic (troubles of the conscious, mental illness, etc.), it is clear that I shall opt for the second approach.

For similar reasons, I shall focus on certain seemingly minor myths in preference to the great and complex cosmogonic myths. I shall choose thematic motifs that seem to illustrate best the elements of my argument, namely, the long ago events that disrupted the order of community life and precipitated a return to chaos, with all that that theme brings with it of terror, dramatic involvement, and anxiety for the individual and collective conscious.

I should like to emphasize that all that is related to confusion and/or disorder has the aspect of tragedy and leads to personality disturbances or even to negation of the individual owing to loss of identity. Chaos, in which all is confounded without distinction or principle, antedates the creation of man, which is, at the same time, the origin of culture. Thus there exists a primordial link between, on the one hand, the theme of "disruption" (or undifferentiation) of cultural relations and signifiers leading to alienation from one another and, on the other hand, disorder of the entire universe. Growing out of this semantic context, the ritual-mythic scenarios "staged" during group healing sessions are an array of pacificatory techniques aimed at bringing order out of pathetic chaos, equated with the primordial reign of terror prior to all really human existence, that is, before the advent of cultural order. In the traditional world, culture unites men while at the same time distinguishing and differentiating them, one from another; it is in this way that it protects the individual from disintegration, from nonrecognition by others, from the loss of self-identity (and hence madness).

We know that in every cultural macrostructure, the symbolic themes concerning life and death are those that, in the end, are at the core of the culture's overall anthropological perspective, because these themes attempt to give form to the crucial questions of man's origin, his ends and his end. No culture escapes these questions. In Black Africa, the various thematic representations of life and death, always indissolubly linked, seem to be animated by the complex play of dialectic complementarity, and it is also against this background that most African myths relating to the origin of misfortune and disease unfold.

The extraordinary richness of this category of myth, as well as its numerous variations throughout the whole of the African continent, proceeds from the perception that death, when it is radical or absolute,[3] is the greatest of all misfortunes. In the face of that experience, which confronts man with the truth of his destiny, myth constitutes a pathetic effort to master death at the symbolic

[3]In Africa, radical death is to die without leaving descendants, which results in the end of the phylogenetic continuum: ancestor — subject — descendant.

level, for in the final analysis, death is interpreted more than it is really explained. In effect, seen as a symbol, it refers to something other than itself. The mythic portrayal of death, like that of suffering with which it is bound up, constitutes an intermediate mode of thinking — neither rational nor irrational. That is why myth accounts for a great many things but does not really explain the one fundamental problem: human suffering. When all is said and done, every attempt succeeds in telling *how* but not in explaining *why*, as if man were unable to account for causal forces outside himself.

From this perspective, one sees how doctors, particularly psychiatrists, are daily confronted with the problem of human suffering (real life), and for this reason their work is necessarily bound up with the world of language (the symbolic). What sort of psychiatrist would not or could not hear his patients' attempts to express the pain they feel? From the beginning, medicine has been anchored in the world of symbols and elemental human meanings. How could it be otherwise? To return to our subject, I maintain that myth, in fixing the origin of suffering, does not give a satisfactory account of it, strictly speaking, but deploys that motif in more or less complex thematic variations, *ad infinitum*. Each culture, each historical period, takes on the thematic variations that it can and/or that it "deserves."

In the anthropological context of Africa, disease and death are thematically portrayed as a relational conflict, a breakdown of communication, an aggressive assault, always evoking the most fundamental symbol of rupture. The essence of human problems, therefore, revolves around the perpetual fear, diffuse but fundamental, of a resurgence of the state of primordial mythic violence (precultural), characterized by a lack of distinction, by undifferentiation, by the absence of stable and well-defined bonds. The features just described give rise to, or account for, the symbolic practices and manipulations aimed at restoring ties in the cultural order. As we shall see in the following pages, most cases involve procedures intended to restore a broken bond (or to create new ones); that is, ultimately, in the order of what we call human, there can be no existence except existence that is socially and culturally linked, and not purely natural. According to African anthropology, from the moment man exists as a human being, he can never be a "natural" being.

At the psychological and sociological levels, I have called attention to the elaboration of the theme of suffering (misfortune, sickness, etc.) as an original feature of the African anthropological perspective. The traditional image of chaotic forces (testifying to a rupture) is repeated at the level of contemporary social reality (individual and collective) in the language of persecution. That is to say that the forces, good or bad, that tradition locates outside the individual nevertheless express a basic human drama, for it is a drama of a relational conflict evoking the primordial symbolism of rupture.

African myths about the origin of death are narratives that bring into play highly symbolic beings; they recount a prototypic or primordial event that was decisive for the present state of man.

To aspire to an exhaustive inventory of thematic variations would be out of the question, in view of the extent of the existing material. Moreover, that is not my purpose here. Such material usually turns up in the form of scattered scraps or fragments that must first be reconstructed in the field through long, laborious, and painstaking work. In this regard, the contributions of Griaule and his colleagues are exemplary (see, for example, Griaule and Dieterlen, 1965). It is Abrahamsson (1951), however, to whom we are indebted for having catalogued — the first to do so, to my knowledge — a considerable number of African mythic themes. And yet, for all that, this undertaking is very difficult, for the material, such as is reported, is still often motley and abridged. For my part, I shall confine myself to consideration of certain themes that are likely to shed some light on the problem under discussion.

First of all, I should like to draw attention to two notions, more or less explicit, that underlie virtually all the narratives to which I shall refer:

1. The withdrawal of God characterizes many traditional themes. A very widespread myth tells how the earth and the sky were contiguous in the beginning, so that God and men then dwelled together.

The withdrawal of God, far from being tantamount to a fall for humans, marks the beginning of religious feeling and, in fact, of the bond with the divine and transcendence through the medium of the ancestors. In effect, it is as if intercourse with the divinity in too direct a fashion ran a constant risk of unavoidable incidents, whence the necessity for establishing a distance, thus making possible a tie in the true sense. One of the direct consequences of this withdrawal of God is the proliferation of intermediaries as a means of access to the divinity. Numerous myths tell of this distancing as well as of the setting up of more directly accessible intercessors in the hierarchy of beings. Only as a last resort does one call on the Supreme Being. The intercessor closest to God is, always, the founding Ancestor.

To summarize, very briefly, from among a number of well-known African anthropological themes I shall single out three symbolic motifs that I hold to be fundamental and that come together, moreover, to form the primary symbolic theme, mentioned earlier, of "rupture" of the bond:

a. *Remoteness:* of God and the founding Ancestor;

b. *Mediation:* concerning mediate communication with the Supreme Being, but also the very common theme of "the message that failed";

c. *Externality:* referring to the relationship of distance with the Supreme Being (God the master); he is not "immediately" present in each individual.

These primordial concepts have their counterpart, of course, in the anthropological structures themselves, consecrated by the Ancestor. Thus hierarchical organization, differentiation, and mediation remain the keystones of communal cultural order.

2. The earth, not the sky, is clearly the setting of visions of blessedness, and it continues to be looked on, everywhere, as the permanent frame of reference. The African's attachment to the soil is, in fact, very deep and well known; in this regard, one could speak of an "obsessive geocentrism" accompanied by a close correspondence between man and the world, the one reflecting the other and vice versa. It would almost seem that man can think of the environment around him only in so far as he can think of himself within that environment.

Such an outlook fosters the creation of a cultural universe, ordered and filled with meanings, which the individual can query at any time to gain knowledge of himself, since both his place and his identity are inconceivable outside this panstructured universe, at the summit of which sits enthroned the founding Ancestor, guarantor, protector, and defender, next to God, of the interests of the community of the living.

I must stress the point, however, that according to African tradition, human beings are essentially terrestrial creatures: God has withdrawn and does not concern himself directly with the affairs of men; on earth, men alone are responsible both for the good and for the evil that may befall them. A Liberian myth (Abrahamsson, 1951, p. 4) marvelously expresses the mutual attraction and bond uniting man and the earth. Sno-Nysoa (the Creator) sent his four sons to earth. When he called them back, they wanted to stay on earth, and the earth, too, wanted to keep them. So God used his "secret power" to bring them back. One morning the eldest did not wake up, and God said to the earth, "I have called him home, but I leave you his body." And so it was done, the way to death was opened as a result of the earth's wish to keep the sons of God.

These features that I have just described — the aloofness of God, the terrestrial nature of man — already suggest that certain themes express (or translate) fundamental choices of the culture. That is why the myths that concern us here are intended not so much to marshal explanations from the outside, strictly speaking, as to provide some insights into the way in which men perceive their present condition. From the outset, mythical narrative raises the problem of the foundations of reality as a whole, by presenting reality as a coherent system of signifiers attached to a fundamental significate. Myth makes the human experience of existence (life, disease, disaster, death, etc.) not an utter absurdity, marked by anguish and disintegration, nor a hardly bearable "natural hazard," but a rational reality that is worth the trouble of living for oneself and for others. In this sense, symbolism, if nothing else, makes possible the unification of individual and collective functions by something that both contains them and transcends them, namely, the Signified.

Numerous myths about the origin of death also describe the reality of living in the course of the story. What clearly emerges from various motifs called upon to justify the coming of death is that death is seen as the inevitable "complement" of life.

An important group of these myths, with a very wide area of distribution, has to do with what writers have come to call the theme of the "message that failed," which I associate with the symbol of mediation. This common theme tells how God sends two animals bearing contradictory messages to mankind, the one bringing tidings of mortality (death) and the other, of immortality (life). After various incidents along the way, the animal bearing the message of eternal life is passed by its fellow bearing the opposite message, so that when the former finally arrives among men, the die has been cast and death is already established on earth.

In this vein, a Zulu myth relates that God sent the chameleon to announce to men that they would not die. But the chameleon is a slow animal, and also it dawdled by eating fruit it found along the way. Some time later God sent the lizard to announce to men that they would die. The lizard darted off like an arrow, was first to arrive, delivered his message to mankind, and was back with God before the chameleon had even reached its destination. Men had accepted the lizard's message and no one could do anything to change it (Parrinder, 1967, p. 56).

Sometimes the conflicting messages are sent by men, when they themselves address their request to God. For example, an Ewe myth tells that men sent a dog to ask God for immortality. But along the way the dog stopped to eat, and a goat, the messenger of mortality, arrived first and told God that men wished to live for a while and then to die. The dog arrived later on, but God had already granted the wish expressed by the goat. And that is how it happened that all men must die (Abrahamsson, 1951, p. 6). The least one can say is that mankind shows great ambivalence in regard to the mortality/immortality duo.

Zahan (1970, pp. 36–44) has analyzed this category of myths with their innumerable variations. In her view, the theme connotes a sharp distinction between the world of God and the world of men. Generally, the message of life is entrusted to a rather slow animal and the message of death to a fast animal. For the world of the living, however, slowness, which is the contrary of action and movement, is associated with death, whereas speed, for converse reasons, is synonymous with life. The incidents the go-betweens meet with along the way serve to account for the semantic reversal of signifiers between the two worlds, so that, in

accepting the "speed" message, men believe that actually they are receiving a symbol of life. Therefore, men
should never forget that symbols bear thinking about,
because they convey a secret, hidden meaning, not
directly accessible.

The attitude of acceptance, even resignation, in the
face of the problem of death, which is found in numerous tales, nevertheless has no connotation of passivity.
It would be much more accurate to see in that acceptance a clearly affirmed wish to justify the present existential order, whatever the price may be. In short, it is
as if the time before the coming of death was an era of
incompletion, of gestation, when rudimentary humans
roamed about in quest of their ontological status. The
advent of death, by assigning a definite configuration to
the indeterminate, brings creation to a conclusion, in a
way, and thrusts man into the axis determined by his
true spatial and temporal coordinates, yet without ir-
revocably cutting him off from the Supreme Being,
since that bond is maintained by the ancestors.

The few examples that follow will serve to illustrate
how the coming of death helped to form the foundations
of life and present-day culture, and will enable us to discern in what basic guises life and death are perceived.

A Luba myth relates that God created first the sun,
then the moon, and finally two human beings — a man
and a woman. He put the two of them in a very large
field where he had planted two banana trees. The trees
grew and bore fruit. One day, one of the humans was
passing by and picked a banana and ate it. When God
asked who had eaten the banana, the humans denied
having done so and they reminded God that they were

not his only creatures. God thereupon summoned the sun and the moon, who also declared they knew nothing about the matter. God then buried the sun in a hole, but the next day, when he looked inside, he found the hole empty. The same thing happened with the moon. Finally, God killed man and put him in the earth, and he remained there forever. Thus God knew that it was man who was guilty (L. de Brandt, cited by Abrahamsson, 1951, p. 49).

This story connects the origin of death to the forbidden consumption of a fruit that happens to be the basic foodstuff of the population in question. Consequently, man finds himself caught between a net and a snare, offering equally fatal outcomes: either he abstains from eating bananas, an indispensable element for his survival, or he eats bananas and his transgression is punished with death, while ensuring him, paradoxically, life.

In either case, man is destined to die. The difference lies only in the significance. If man opts for the second alternative, it is because it permits him, in a way, to confront death in order to survive, to "choose" his death, to give it meaning, and to assert himself through an intentional act — defying a blind determinism over which he would have no control. His mortal sin finds its justification in that it marks a paradigmatic act,[4] establishing the basis of a future culture.

Other functions essential to life are also called on to account for death. According to a Ngala myth, Nkengo

4The term paradigmatic is used here in the theological sense and not in the sense given it by modern linguists.

had seen how men were dying every day in great numbers. One day, he called up to the Cloud Folk, asking them to throw him down a rope, which they did. Nkengo grasped the rope and was pulled up to them. Once there, he first had to wait for a day and a night. The following day the Cloud Folk said to him, "You came here to seek eternal life and escape from death. Your request cannot be heard for seven days, but in the meantime you must not go to sleep." Nkengo was able to sit awake for six days, but on the seventh he fell asleep. The people of Cloud Land became angry and threw him back to earth. Then he told men how he had failed in warding off sleep and how he had been driven away with these words: "Be gone with your dying; you shall not have eternal life, and every day there will be death among you!" Men made fun of him for having tried to conquer eternity and having fallen asleep. And this is why there is still death on earth (Abrahamsson, 1951, p. 36).

In the last example, death exists from the very beginning. It is a *de facto* state awaiting institutionalization. Immortality is the stake in a test of staying awake for a prolonged period, in which the hero, a Promethean fool exposed to the ridicule of his peers, eventually fails. The fact is the ordeal runs counter to his vital need for restorative rest, which at the same time is the symbolic equivalent of death.

I should like to point out that the two opposing pairs — wakefulness-immortality on the one hand, sleep-death on the other hand — are always associated in the symbolism of mythic thinking: "Sleep is the messenger of death" (Pare proverb); "Death is one with sleep"

(Bushman proverb). Moreover, prolonged sleeplessness
is one of the classic trials of initiation rituals.[5]

It would seem that, in the final analysis, immortality
cannot be conceptualized other than indirectly through
attributes contrary to those of mortality (negative definition).

Whereas immortality follows the course of a continuous line (connoting perpetual wakefulness), mortality appears as a rhythmic succession of alternating
wakefulness and unconsciousness. By blotting out con-
sciousness and memory, sleep removes man from immediate social life, just as death removes him from
organic life. Even more, the "absence from the world"
inherent in sleep implies temporary oblivion to the primordial wisdom governing the destiny of the community; hence it follows that the sleeper, like the madman or
the transgressor, embodies a potential threat of attack
on the cultural order along with a resurgence of the initial, precultural chaos.

The twofold problem of alternation and duration
posed by the symbolism of sleep is found in another
large category of myths, from which I offer the following example.

According to the Luba, when Kabezya-Mpungu
created the world, he placed one man and two women
on earth. He then gave the man a knife and a hoe and
commanded him to hew, weave, forge, and hunt.

[5]During initiation to the Ghetshogo Bwiti among the Mitsogo of central
Gabon, the neophytes are kept in a state of prolonged wakefulness, for
seven consecutive days and nights, with the help of taking *iboga* (a plant
that has stimulant, narcotic, or hallucinogenic effects, depending on the
dosage used).

He gave the same tools to the women and told them to till the fields, cook, make baskets, and so on. These first human beings lived happily until one of the women began to grow old. But Kabezyu-Mpungu had foreseen that and had given her the power to grow young again and the possibility, if she succeeded the first time, of preserving that gift for herself and her fellow creatures. So when the woman started to age, she took her companion's winnowing basket and shut herself in her hut. There she began to peel off all her old skin (which came off without difficulty), placing the shreds in the basket. As she did so, a new skin emerged, as fresh as that of a baby. The operation was almost finished when the other woman entered the hut to get her winnowing basket. The moment she opened the door, the rejuvenated woman fell dead, taking her secret with her. For this reason everyone must now die, and since that time Kabezyu-Mpungu no longer concerns himself with his creatures directly (Abrahamsson, 1951, p. 61).

The numerous variations built up around this central motif can be reduced to an underlying pattern. In the beginning, men did not die but grew young again, either by changing their skin like a snake, or by rising from their grave, the same as the moon, which returns every night. The clumsiness, indiscretion, or ill will of some member of the first family is the cause of one procedure or another — depending on the case — being disrupted in the course of its performance, making periodic rejuvenation impossible forever after.

The idea that death is not a radical severance but a cyclical, biological episode belongs to a large category of myth concerning cosmic renewal and circular time.

That particular way of apprehending time, however, which in many respects is satisfactory for other systems of thought, is inadequate from the African point of view, for an African could not conceive of time without the vital medium of the succession of generations. In the African anthropological perspective, circular time does not seem to be "humanized" time, in the sense that its corollary, periodic rejuvenation, would result in the blockage, then dissolution of age classes, and consequently diachronic chaos (violent because of its negation of society as such). Thus there is a need to adopt some other temporality, the concept of time as experienced: time lived by the elders, time lived by those who are younger, distinguishing the successive generations and hence making for a highly social temporality. Interruption by a third party results in disrupting the order of things, that is, in confounding those two scales of vertical time and jumbling them together in a linear (horizontal) time, spatializing time and therefore depriving it of meaning. Thus there can be no purely "natural," biological time without a base of concrete human groups to give it substance and reality.

An event of such far-reaching importance as the confounding of temporal systems in a flat and linear scale not only gives evidence of conflictual violence, precisely as means and prime mover, but *is* violence, especially since the confusion is so great and the change so radical in nature. This is why in the various accounts the disruptive third party is, at base, always presented as motivated by feelings of ill will (spite, hate, jealousy, etc.), which, in this context, are also antisocial emotions. It is true that some versions — like the one just related, in fact — seem to attribute the sudden arrival of the unwanted spectator to "chance" or "inadvertence," for example. We should not let ourselves be deceived, however, by the seeming innocuousness of such an act in terms of intention. Myth delights in disguising or minimizing the essential core of its truth. But in the ushering in of "disorder," there are no "innocent" acts, for innocence or inadvertence could mean that the disorder of natural law presides over the destinies of men. Thus there is no fundamental difference between absent-mindedness, carelessness, and violence. Or perhaps it would be better to say that their apparent difference disappears in the convergence of their consequences. For proof we need only turn to the numerous myths in which the direct cause of death is thoughtlessness, forgetfulness, or negligence — so many forms of carelessness that are equally likely to do damage to that delicate and complex web of distinctions, identifications, and correspondences on which all social order rests.

In the traditional world, all conduct has a meaning, and indeed that is why it is conduct rather than behavior. Man, quite literally, is coexistent with the meaningful. With remarkable intuition, traditional African thought equates violence with confusion due to the nondifferentiation of beings and things (resulting in lack of identification). Hence there is a concern, almost obsessional, to fix the precise identity of everyone and at the same time to maintain the differential distance that distinguishes everyone, for the dissolution of that distance risks bringing on what Girard (1972) calls a "sacrificial crisis," which is defined as the collapse of the cultural order as a whole in the uncontrolled reciprocal violence of brothers turned implacable enemies from then on.

A radical obliteration of differences leading to a loss of individual identity is therefore always bound up with violence and conflict, which accounts for the capital importance attached to such mental activities as classifying, differentiating, associating, and contrasting in order to avoid confusion. Numerous myths relate the origin of death to a failure to recognize, or the absence of, differential series as well as hierarchical and classificatory distinctions.

In the beginning, a Serer tradition relates, human beings did not die. The first creature to die was a dog. It was buried in a termite hill at the foot of a baobab tree, in a place called *Lui m'bay fa* (the grave of the dog). Since no one had ever seen such a thing, a big ceremony was made of it: the women wept, the dead dog was wrapped in a beautiful cloth, and so on. When God (Koh) found out about it, he was very angry at all that fuss made over a dog, and as a consequence, he decided that death should also be the lot of human beings (Tastevin, cited by Abrahamsson, 1951, p. 100).

The life of present-day man is predicated on a clear distinction between the world of human beings and that of animals. Death is the concomitant of confusion between these two categories of living creatures. That distinction is particularly crucial and difficult for the following reasons:

1. Animals are in fact very close to man. They live near him, are the focus of many of his activities, and

serve as food for him. Certain pastoral peoples stress this closeness, going so far as to make their herds a systematic replica of their own social structure.

2. This same closeness, otherwise disavowed, gives an animal its value as a substitute sacrifice, in so far as it is for ritual purposes (ritual victimization).

A Lala myth provides a clear insight into man's relations of correspondence and identification with animals. Before dying, an old wizard bequeathed his herd to his son. He also left him a little box, commanding him not to open it. If the son obeyed, his herd would prosper and he would live a long time. But the son's wife, like all women, was curious and insisted that the box be opened. Two tsetse flies escaped from it. The man succeeded in catching one, but the other killed his whole herd and became "the ancestress of this pest" (Hughes, cited by Abrahamsson, 1951, p. 45).

It is interesting to note that in this account, the punishment of death does not strike man directly, but rather his herd. I should like to hazard the following interpretation: transgression has the immediate effect of doing away with the barrier between man and animal so that they become interchangeable, thus opening the breach to misfortune, which strikes indiscriminately. Through allusion, the tale suggests that the blow initially directed at man's herd falls back on man himself, by describing the tsetse fly as the ancestress of a terrifying scourge whose rapid proliferation is equaled only by the contagiousness of intragroup sacrificial crisis.

Perplexity in the face of death and the inadequacy of the actions taken on its first appearance frequently combine to divert death from its original, supposedly transitory, mission. For example, according to the Bena

Kanioka, when men saw someone dying, they laughed and organized festivities instead of observing the rules that would have warded off death. In other accounts, men were chastised for having neglected to bury the first dead person.

In this second version, the men described in the myths were ignorant of burial, a practice that confirms the separation between the world of the dead and that of the living. Once again, the unfortunate confounding of those two normally distinct realms sets in motion the drama from which the protagonists cannot escape.

All these prescribed practices, all the rules, prohibitions, and codes of conduct that mythology seeks to justify, are ultimately aimed at conveying the following message: cultural cohesion and order rest on a subtle and delicate system of differential identification of one and all. Let certain elements of the overall system be disturbed, and ties are ruptured; that is enough for the whole edifice to collapse, bringing with it, in its fall, the dissolution of all cultural structures and institutions, including those of the family, which formerly provided everyone protection, security, and warmth in the traditional milieu. Therefore man must be thoughtful, alert, and respectful toward others within the complex web of community relations in order to share in the common responsibility for his destiny and that of others. Underlying this attitude is not only traditional group unity but also, on a broader anthropological level, the rejection (or distrust) of natural or so-called objective law, which, when it comes to preside over human destinies, is invariably one with violence and intracommunity conflict, as testified to by all these myths.

Death can be the stake (a fearsome price) in some

competition, or it may simply be the consequence of an unlucky choice. According to the Dogon, Amma (God) told men to choose between two mats: one was the mat of captivity, the other the mat of death. They refused the mat of captivity, and when they lay down on the other, they began to die (Abrahamsson, 1951, p. 43).[6]

A Dogon myth relates, for its part, that death was a being named Fi. In the beginning, he was not aware of the existence of men, and when he saw them for the first time, he was greatly frightened and feared that they might kill him. He went to find the toad and the frog, thinking that if he were to succeed in killing one of them, he would prove that he was more powerful than men. Fi thereupon dug a hole in the ground and dared the two animals to jump over it. If they succeeded, no evil would befall them, but if they failed, they and all creatures living on earth would know death. The frog, which has such long legs and is a good jumper, wanted to try first, but the toad prevented the frog from doing so and jumped first himself, so awkwardly that he fell in the hole. When the toad implored Fi to let him out, Fi refused and said, "Thus you are going to die, and thus will all men die and be put in the ground like you." And men take vengeance on toads by crushing them whenever they find one in their path (Vergiat, cited by Abrahamsson, 1951, pp. 8-9).

Girard (1972) writes that "human violence is always presented as external to man; that is why it is merged and confounded in the sacred with forces that truly

---

[6] This is but a tiny facet of the great Dogon myth that has been recorded in its entirety by Griaule and his colleagues (cf. Griaule and Dieterlen, 1965).

press heavily on man from the outside — death, disease, natural phenomena . . ." (p. 122).

I should like to present here an account that provides an excellent illustration of the persecution theme that underlies the idea — a common traditional notion — that death is never natural but always occurs as the result of some mistake by a human or nonhuman creature:

> A story from the Mbundu of Angola tells of two brothers, one of whom, Ngunza, had a dream while he was away from home that his brother had died. When he got back he demanded who had killed his brother, and his mother said it was Death. He vowed to fight Death, and got a blacksmith to make a great iron trap.
>
> He set this in the bush, watched it with great vigilance, and successfully caught Death. Death pleaded with Ngunza to let him go, but he refused, saying that Death was always killing people. Death denied this, alleging that people died by their own fault or that of somebody else, and if Ngunza would release him he could visit his land and see for himself. Ngunza consented and four days later they set off for the family of the dead. Death told him to watch the new arrivals, and of each one he asked what had killed them. Some said it was their own vanity, others jealous husbands, and so on. They had all died through the fault of some human being, and so it was unfair to blame Death [Parrinder, 1967, p. 63].

A final, more complex account of the origin of death will serve to introduce, through the themes it brings in, another broad category of myths concerning blood sacrifice (at the base of the present cultural order) and the ritual commemoration of this primordial event.

The Krachi of Togo relate that long, long ago there was a great famine in the world. A young man who had set out to seek food came to a strange and unfamiliar place in the forest. There he found a giant lying on the ground, with hair so long that it reached from Krachi to Salaga. The young man asked the giant to give him some food, and the giant agreed to so do on condition that the youth stay and be his servant. The young man agreed in turn, but after serving the giant for a while, he wanted to go home. The giant, whose name was Owuo, or Death, consented, provided that another servant be sent to him. And so the young man sent his brother. The famine continued, however, and after a while the young man became hungry again and began to miss the giant's good food. So he went back to Owuo to serve him but was surprised after a few days at never seeing his brother. The giant declared that a special task was keeping the boy away. Once again the young man became homesick, and the giant let him leave, but asked this time that a girl be sent to him, for he wanted to get married. The young man persuaded his sister to agree to this, and she departed, accompanied by a servant girl. The famine was still severe, however, and once again the youth returned to Owuo's dwelling place. The giant received him with ill humor, but nevertheless allowed him to enter and eat. The young man began eating on a bone and discovered with horror that it had belonged to his sister. He looked around him and saw that all the meat there was the flesh of his sister and her servant girl.

He fled, running all the way home, and told the whole village what he had seen. A council was held to debate what course to follow, and it was decided that they would go into the forest and set fire to the giant's long hair, which was so abundant that it covered all the surrounding region. They did so and then, keeping their distance, they watched the giant, who shook his head and sweated more and more as the flames approached, until they finally enveloped his head and he seemed to be dead. In the ashes of his hair, near the roots, a packet containing a magic medicine was found, and when this was strewn on the bone of the brother, the sister, and the servant girl, they all came back to life. Someone suggested sprinkling a little medicine on the giant, but the others protested, fearing he might revive. Nevertheless, the youth let a little of the powder fall into the giant's eye. At once, the eye opened, and everyone fled in terror. But it is from that eye that death comes, for from that time forward Owuo has lived among human beings, and every time he opens and closes that eye, someone dies. And unfortunately for us, he never stops blinking (Cardinall, cited in Abrahamsson, 1951, p. 83).

Let us review the various themes and follow the thread of this fascinating tale. The community is in a state of crisis (famine). Far from the village, at a most remote spot, there is a giant, a monstrous double whose long hair, covering the countryside, might evoke the growth and spread of seeds of dissension at the very doorstep of the society in crisis. The most elementary prudence would suggest maintaining and reinforcing the separation between these two antithetical regions to stave off an explosive onslaught.

A young man, however, strikes the first blow at the isolation of these two worlds by going from one to the other. He asks the giant for food, or, in other words, from the outset he identifies the giant as source and solution of the misfortune the community is suffering, namely, famine. For the time being, however, the crisis is still building: the differential structure is unsteady but still holds, resisting the onslaught that would bring explosion. The young man nevertheless continues to go back and forth between the two zones, each time blurring their frontiers a little more, contaminating one with the other, reinforcing their interpenetration with terrible alliances. Finally the crisis reaches its paroxysm. Within the group, which has been undermined and is disintegrating, the latent conflict is seeking a locus of investment. It is then that, bursting like a bomb, the accusation of cannibalism is brought against the giant, and instantly all the arguments in which the group was perishing are polarized and converge on him. To use Girard's (1972) terminology, the lost unanimity is re-formed around a scapegoat. By common accord, the members of the community march together on the giant and set his hair on fire, which quickly becomes a blazing inferno, representing the wild and sudden culmination of the crisis.

The giant's death heralds the resolution of the crisis and the beginning of an era of prosperity for the community. And, indeed, those are the favorable consequences of the collective immolation: order is re-established, the famine is checked (the giant's dwelling was overflowing with food), social structures are restored and imbued with fresh vigor. Better still, at the very spot where the sacrifice was consummated (near the roots of the hair), the men in the myth find a miraculous medicine. Thus the blood sacrifice of the monstrous double will have had the twofold effect of reviving the cultural order and imparting a new knowledge capable of combating disease and death.

The tale should normally have stopped there, but it nonetheless continues to develop its lesson even further. Before changing into an inexhaustible source of blessings, the victim had become the focal point of confusion, hatred, rivalry, in short, of all the conflicts that were "doing in" the society in crisis. Skipping to the end of the story, we find a veritable reversal with respect to the scheme of things at the beginning. Before the crisis, men are immortal because the strict separation they maintain between their world and the "other" world enables them to save themselves from it. The thread of the narrative leads, at the end, to an assimilation (confounding) of the two initially distinct zones and, as a result, to the presence of an implacable monster among men, one that must be paid tribute with life in a coexistence of constant dread. This example alone enables us to discern one of the functions of prohibitions and taboos, which is to classify, to distinguish, to separate — in short, to identify special preserves without confounding them and to isolate potentially explosive points in the community edifice.

Lastly, I should like to point out that the sacrifice of a primordial giant is a theme frequently found in agrarian cultures. The dismembered body of the primeval sacrificial victim is supposed to have given rise to vegetable species, an event that is sometimes ritually reenacted in the hope of increasing the yield of the harvest.

The origin of this type of ogre is often mysterious: all that is known is that he appeared on earth after the creation of the world and that his immolation contributed to (and coincided with) the condition of present-day men, either by radically changing their way of living or by initiating them to some practical knowledge vital to the community. In the tradition of some peoples, initiation rituals are directly inspired by such a primordial murder.[7]

This is true of the secret society of the Mandja and the Bande. According to the myth told when the neophytes are initiated, Ngakola lived on earth at one time. He had a very black body covered with long hair. No one knew where he came from, but he lived in the bush. He had the power to kill a man and bring him back to life. He told the men, "Send me people. I shall eat them and vomit them up renewed!" They followed his advice, but since Ngakola returned only half of those whom he swallowed, the men decided to slay him. They gave him large quantities of manioc to eat into which they had mixed stones, thus weakening the monster so that they could kill him with knives and spears. This myth forms the basis of and accounts for the rituals of the secret society. A flat stone plays an important role in the initiation ceremonies. According to tradition, this consecrated, hierophantic stone was taken from Ngakola's body. A neophyte is taken into a hut that symbolizes the monster's body. There he hears Ngakola's lugubrious voice, and there he is whipped and subjected to torture,

---

[7] A task of future African researchers will be to systematically collect elemental themes of this sort.

for he is told that he has now entered Ngakola's belly and is being digested. The other initiates chant in chorus: "Ngakola, take the entrails of all of us! Ngakola, take the liver of all of us!" After other ordeals have been braved, the initiation master finally announces that Ngakola, who had eaten the neophyte, has given him back (E. Andersson cited by Eliade, 1957, p. 273).

The elements of this ritual-mythic complex can be reconstructed as follows: A supernatural being, who has come from a secret place under mysterious circumstances, "swallows" men in order to bring them back to a higher existence — none other than initiation. But men fail to recognize the import of this initiatory death, and they slay the monster, perhaps to take over his power as a group. Later, this primeval murder forms the basis of the initiation ritual itself, a ceremony that transforms "natural" man (a child) into "cultural" man (an adult), by deliberate orientation of all the constituent elements of his personality toward community values.

Thus the formative action of primeval violence is such a constant, running through a multitude of varying themes, that it should be reinserted in the culture of mythical chronology. In their thematic scenarios, cosmogonic myths postulate the prior existence of an undifferentiated subreality, represented by chaos, androgyny or the primordial egg, etc. The separation of the sky and earth usually marks the cosmogonic act and the first distinction made in the original state of undifferentiation. Myths of origin form an extension of the cosmogony and bring creation to completion either through: *hierogamy* (sacred marriage), an event ritually reenacted in orgy (which symbolizes regression to primeval chaos) or in ceremonial union; or *sacrifice* (immolation of a victim), an act commemorating creation that is continued by men, with that creation marking the beginning of contemporary civilization.

Sacrifice is recreative in the sense that, as we have seen, the sacrificial victim emerges in striking fashion as a unifying focus for differences, that is, as a pacifier. That is why the primordial victim survives in rites in which the murder is periodically commemorated in collective fashion, and that is also precisely what myths recall to mind.

In a number of narratives, the primordial victim is very clearly an ancestor who has broken all the prohibitions, has sown death and destruction all around him, and is himself killed in turn, thus preparing the way for the coming of a new order. Such is the case of Nkongolo, a cruel, incestuous, and drunken king whose exploits are related in Bantu epic poetry, and who became, after he had been killed, the first sacred king of the Luba of Zaïre.

The rites preceding the enthronement of certain traditional monarchs are derived from legends of primeval exploits. In a number of countries, for example, before the king-to-be is invested, he is obliged to ritually violate the most revered prohibitions of the community, especially the incest taboo — a negation of all differences. All his misdeeds — supreme violence — serve to make him detestable in the eyes of his future subjects at the time of the investiture ceremonies. And meanwhile, his subjects shower him with all sorts of ill-treatment and harassment; they abuse him, upbraid him, and so on. But behind this ritual-mythic scenario can be discerned the sacrificial pattern: precisely by making himself guilty of such terrible deeds, the future ruler is expressly marked as a scapegoat, whose ritual immolation will transform all the individual and social conflicts that have become centered on his person, making him a source of peace, stability, and prosperity for one and all. The ritual of investiture will culminate in the blood sacrifice of a substitute animal, which is viewed as a reenactment of the collective slaying of the first mythical king (at the same time it represents, as we have seen, the symbolic execution of the king being invested). As soon as the ceremonies are over, however, the king will assume a special status, and throughout his reign he will have all the characteristics of inviolability and respect appropriate to divinity.

Therefore all these ritual-mythic practices and institutions, of which we have covered only a few brief but significant examples, ultimately converge on one and the same meaning: to wit, that all human drama should be remembered (myth) and should be related by a cultural link of repetition (ritual) to the primordial drama of creation as the foundation for the coming of the current cultural order. From the point of view of society, then, evil consists in the threat of a resurgence of the old chaos, prior to creation, and hence to culture and sociocultural bonds — that is, to humankind. For it challenges not only man's freedom but his very existence. That is why man will try to circumscribe such a threat by delineating areas in which the sacred tolerates no intrusion and by defining prohibitions whose violation brings misfortune. In my opinion, the meaning of prohibition, expressed overtly or covertly in mythical accounts, can be characterized as a respect for law and the avoidance of confusion. It is, at base, a formal inter- diction of any exercise — which would be a purely pri- vate repetition — of violence, because it would take the community as a whole back to precultural conditions and plunge the existence of everyone into total anarchy.

Rites have deep meaning only within a well-defined cultural community, whereas obsessional ritual — which is not of the essence or spiritual in nature, which is not related to what the community holds sacred, which is cut off from the primordial symbols made vivid in the traditional sacred narratives — can be accurately described as purely psychological and/or psychopathological, and seems to me to be ape-like. Therefore obsessional ritual is fundamentally different from sacred ritual in the true sense, because they do not, in my opinion, have the same structure. In effect, what is signified for the neurotic is buried in his individuality and, in the final analysis, "doubles" or duplicates his narcissistic desire, which functions as if he were his own end in himself. For man confronting the sacred, how- ever, what is signified is the Word, Law, Tradition — in short, man's Origin, in the sacrifice of the founding Ancestor, creator of the Law, guarantor of peace and coexistence among present-day human beings.

At the founding of every new cultural tradition (establishment of a culture being establishment of a truth that creates new values), the community in crisis (the phase of precultural chaos) will follow a sacrificial pattern. It will attempt to circumscribe and then "expel" conflictual intracommunity configurations of

violent relations by crystallizing them (through sacrificial "victimization") on the Enemy, the Persecutor
(e.g., the monster of the mythic theme just described),
whose presence, visible or invisible but always immanent, is felt deep down to be the threat or, even worse, a
major impediment to the establishment of a new community harmony. One comes to see more clearly that
current conflicts are in essence bound up with events
that took place in the beginning and are related in
mythic themes. Similarly, one can better understand — in terms of African psychological anthropology — that the double (the Enemy) comes under the
heading of active negative in the three-dimensional
structure that defines, precisely, the elements that go to
make up the person/personality.

Traditional accounts give us various symbolic representations of this double in the form of aggressive antisocial beings: monster, genie, enemy brother, etc., of
which the *suntubon*[8] happens to be the most dangerous.
The latter is perceived as the prime destroyer of the innermost substance of the person/personality, and is
firmly aligned, in terms of social and cultural representation, on the side of evil and darkness. These witches
are thought to cause the disintegration of the personal
essence of individual beings and, in so doing, to sap and
destroy the basic elements of the community as a whole.
According to Parrinder (1967, p. 92), the Hausa tell a
story of a female witch who had nine mouths on her

---

[8] For a discussion of the term *suntubon* see I. Sow, 1977, pp. 212-214.
"Witch" or "sorcerer" in the sense of African sorcery designates a
malevolent being capable of destroying — at a distance, by purely psychic
means — the central core of his victim's personality.

body, but these mouths, of course, remained invisible. One day she went to the forest to gather leaves from a certain tree, and then boiled them to make some broth for her husband and his father. The husband uncovered his bowl, and the broth immediately called out in a threatening tone, "Cover me up, or else you shall die." The husband's father uncovered his bowl in turn, and the broth called out to him, "Cover me up, or else you shall die." The husband thereupon seized his own bowl as well as his father's and threw them both at his wife's head. Instantly the nine mouths appeared and she was exposed as a witch, so she had to run off pell-mell.

Zahan (1970, pp. 96-97) reports that among the Bambara, sorcerers are the only beings in creation who do not possess a *dya* (i.e, a double). This is why they seek to destroy members of their own family, then other people, by manducation (which in this case means consuming the vital personal essence rather than the bodily covering of their victims); indeed, they capture precisely what they are lacking, namely, the *dya* of their victims.

Less dangerous are the genies, which are personifications of obscure natural forces that are not easy to control. As I have already indicated, in the traditional way of thinking the world is a universe, that is, an "orderly" world, organized according to hierarchical meanings that are recapitulated in a coherent system of symbols. The Mende of Sierra Leone, in west Africa, tell how communication between God, man, and nature came to be established in the universe.

> At first men did not pray, but they came to the Supreme Being with small complaints. God con-

sidered how he could make men know his will.[9] He
created a mountain and gave it the ability to talk to
men, thinking that if men were used to the voice of
the mountain, and kept its laws, they would also
hear the divine voice and laws. He also gave men
the power of dreaming.

One night an old man had a dream in which he
saw the mountain coming to him as an old man and
calling him friend, saying that he must tell the
village chief to get his people to bring food for the
mountain to eat. The dreamer asked where the old
man had come from and he answered that he came
from the mountain. The dreamer looked towards
the mountain and saw that it had disappeared, and
the old man said that was because he was the
mountain. After the old man had gone away the
mountain could be seen again. When the old man
awoke he told the chief about his dream. All the
people were assembled, the story was told, and it
was agreed to give food to the mountain. But they
told the old man to ask the mountain for help to
catch the animal that would be needed for food. So
he went with his sons, picking up twenty stones on
the way.

At the foot of the mountain he cleared a space
and called out to the mountain that if it really did
need food it must arrange the stones so that it could

---

[9] One sees unfolding here the theme of God's withdrawal and remoteness
as well as that of possible mediation between man and God. Among the
means of drawing closer to God are speech, prayer, and dreams; but as
always in Africa, any dialogue between God and man is carried on through
the privileged intercession of the ancestors.

be known how many animals were needed. The dreamer and his sons went home, but next morning they came back and found the stones set out in order. Nine stones faced the mountain, and that meant that nine animals would escape. Ten stones were facing the man and so ten would be killed. One stone was in the middle and that animal must be kept alive till sacrificed by the dreamer. This was done when the men went hunting. Then the village men collected rice, salt and palm-oil from their women and took them with the meat to the mountain. The women were sent back because there was not enough food for them. The live animal was sacrificed, and meat, rice and oil were put on leaves. The dreamer took a kola nut, which splits into halves and is a sign of friendship. He called on the mountain to show whether the food had been received and appreciated, and tossing the halves of the kola nut into the air he let them fall to the ground. They fell with their white side facing upwards, a sign of acceptance. This was done four times, and the sign of acceptance always appeared.

The dreamer asked the mountain to protect the town against warfare, save women in childbirth, protect children against witchcraft, heal all who were sick, and care for the people as they had cared for the mountain. Every year the mountain was a place of prayer for men, and they brought gifts to it. But God had pity on the women who were not allowed to share in the sacrifice. He told a woman in a dream to pray at a great rock, and since then men and women have prayed at mountains and rocks, and also at trees and rivers [Parrinder, 1967, pp. 66–67].

This mythical tale also takes account of what I have described elsewhere as the vertical dimension of the ego: the axis that leads to the special domain of ancestral tradition (the sphere of the sacred). It tells how the ancestors who were the founders of tradition, of the word that established the present order of cultural coexistence, made alliances long ago with the masters of the natural world (now represented by local genies and other spirits). It indicates by what means (offerings, sacrifices) communication and coexistence should be strengthened and maintained, as well as how the power of the natural world can be tamed or transformed into a benevolent force, to the profit of the entire community. For these reasons, besides the classical opposition between nature and culture, there is also room for possible alliance and complementarity.

By the same token, from that time forward nature, as such, ceased to be totally hostile to man, thanks to all the intermediaries that have special relationships with the ancestors (at the time of the transition from pre-cultural nature to the culture proper of today). These privileged intermediaries are also the focus of important prohibitions and of respect on the part of contemporary men. African tradition is rich in sacred alliances of this sort, sealed in far-off times. It will suffice to mention the following examples:

1. The sacred python of the Fon (at Whydah in Dahomey) is called Tohuiyo, or "the one the ancestors respected."

2. The sacred elephant of the Samake clan (of Mali) recalls that the clan's ancestor entered into contact with the invisible thanks to an old solitary elephant.

3. Bambara tradition relates that the ancestor of the Diarra clan, in Mali, was initiated by a toothless old lion without claws (indeed, Diarra means "lion").

4. The Moslem prohibition against eating pork is reinterpreted by a Dogon tale that asks, "Do you know why Moslems [in this case their Peul neighbors] don't eat pork? It is because once there was a Peul out on the plain who was almost dead from thirst when he saw a pig in front of him. He ran after the pig and it led him to water, and so he could drink. For this reason Moslems must never kill a pig or, even less, eat one."

5. The hippopotamus revered by the Baoule harbors a similar symbolic meaning. Long ago, when the Baoule were at war and being pursued by their enemies, they suddenly came to a river they were unable to cross, for there was no bridge. They then turned to a "wise man" to find a solution to the problem, and he announced that if they wanted to cross the river, the child of Abla Pokou, who was the village chief's own sister, would have to be thrown into the water. And the mother consented to sacrifice her son to obtain the help of the water spirits. When the child was thrown into the river, the people saw hippopotamuses rise up in the water and form a bridge, so that the Baoule could cross over and reach the savanna. Later, some Baoule settled in the country of Akissi Faa, and one of their descendants founded the village where the people who have preserved this traditional account live today (I should like to note that *Ba* means child and *oule* means both to die

and to be born, and it was precisely the sacrifice of the child that enabled the Baoule to escape their pursuers and survive).

Myths and legendary epics of similar import abound everywhere in Black Africa. In such narratives, what is emphasized is the prominent and central role of the founding Ancestor in the creation of culture and indeed, by that very fact, in the taming of nature to the benefit of human beings, his spiritual descendants.

I shall conclude this brief review of traditional African themes with the Fang[10] story of the separation related by Cendrars (1921), a tale that contains the principal thematic elements we have just examined.

Once upon a time, long, long ago, there were not very many men, and they lived peacefully together with the animals in one big village where Ndun had charge of everything. Ndun settled conflicts wisely, for he was "old and prudent," and the Creator himself was not above coming to pay him homage. But one day discord erupted among the women, between the old ones and the young ones.

The young women accused their elders of loading them with too much work in the fields, but their husbands said they were wrong, and so did Ndun. That is why the young women decided to seek revenge. In the morning all the women went to fetch water at the spring, but the young ones got there ahead of the old ones, and after having filled their jars, they bathed

[10] The Fang and the Fang-Beti group, a very important cluster with a rich sociocultural tradition, occupy a geographic area that includes, among other regions, northwest Gabon, Equatorial Guinea, and northeast Cameroon.

and frolicked in the spring, so that the old women could offer their husbands only cloudy and muddy water.

The narrative continues:

> The old women were spiteful in the evening, and the young women still more spiteful in the morning. . . .
>
> And soon blows were falling right and left: Yi, yi, yi! Kwas, kwas! Yi, yi! The jars went flying, blood ran down. . . . Things could not go on this way. Every day, fresh quarrels, every day more blows. And soon, naturally, the men joined in. The young ones took the part of the young, the old ones were some for the old and some for the young.
>
> The chief of the village said: "This can't go on any longer!"
>
> All the women thought the same. . . . Particularly as the women, both young and old, lost all their time making new jars to take the place of those they broke. To get the right clay for making pottery they had to go a long, long way. The men were ill-pleased, and the women more annoyed still [Cendrars, 1921, pp. 23–25].

To summarize the course of events, the old chief called the men together to discuss matters, and after a long palaver, a solution was decided on but it proved to be inadequate for resolving the conflict. So Ndun went to Nzame, God the Creator,[11] and in the morning, after spending the night together, the two of them

---

[11] Ndun, the wise old man and head of the community, would become the founding Ancestor, in close communication with Nzame, God the Creator, one and all-powerful.

made their way toward the village, where the Creator witnessed the quarreling that took place at the spring. He then ordered that the horn be sounded to call together the whole village, men as well as women.

> Nzame spoke: "It is I who command all things. . . . And I have come to put peace in the midst of my children. . . . This, then, is what I shall do. . . . You have become too many to live together on the same hillside; moreover you have disobeyed me. I said to you: "Live in peace and without quarreling. You have not obeyed me."
>
> Here the men interrupted, crying: "It was the women who disobeyed!"
>
> But Nzame silenced them. "Be silent, I am the master! Man is man, woman is woman. You will therefore part. Some will go to the right, the others to the left. Some will go forward, the others will turn backward, and you will remain at peace."
>
> But the old man Ndun, the chief of the race, felt great sorrow in his heart on hearing these words and he fell down backward and was as one dead. His wives wept and began the funeral lamentations, but Nzame said: "I have taken Ndun to myself; since he is your father, he must remain with us. I am the master of life and of death" [Cendrars, 1921, pp. 27–28].

The Creator repeated his order to the people to separate from one another and to take with them the dog and the hen. Then he told those assembled to go home and sleep, and the next day the people saw two things that happened:

The first was this. On entering his hut Ndun, the father of the race, felt a chill in his heart, for his people were about to leave him. . . . The next day, he was cold all over, and his wives said: "He is dead." Nzame said: "I know. I am the master of life. I am the master of death. I have taken Ndun. Perform the funeral rites."

. . . After the death chant the Creator commanded: "Take two wives, an old one and a young one."

They took them. And the Creator said: "Let the blood flow, for I am the master."

They let their blood flow, and they died. And when they were dead the Creator said: "Dig a deep hole."

The dug a deep hole. Then the Creator said: Lay Ndun at the bottom."

And when he was laid there he said: "Now burn the two wives." And they burned them.

And when they were burned the Creator said: "This is called sacrifice. And thus you shall do again when I command you, for I am the master."

And they all answered: "Thou art the master, yea."

Nzame said once more: "It is well. Take the ashes and keep them always with you. It is the sign of mystery. I will protect you."

. . . And when they had danced the funeral dances the Creator spoke again. "On the night that Ndun died, what beast did you see in your dreams?" And each of them had seen a beast, for so Nzame had willed it.

Each man therefore named an animal, and

Nzame said: "It is well."

He lifted his finger, saying only: "I wish!" And the animals came running, one of each kind. And each animal took its place beside each man, according as each had dreamed.

The Creator said: "Let their blood flow." Each man took his sacrificial knife and cut the throat of his animal; the blood flowed and flowed and covered the hillside [Cendrars, 1921, pp. 29–30].

The story then tells how some men did not have an animal but had each seen a tree in their dreams. One tree of each kind was cut down, and again in accordance with Nzame's instructions, the wood was heaped up and animals were placed on top of the pile. The Creator then made a sign, and Lightning, Thunder, and Fire made their first appearance on earth. And men sang the Fire Song. Then the animals were burned, and their charred bones were ground to powder and mixed with the ashes of Ndun. Each man received his share. And the Creator said:

"This is your sign of brotherhood."

...After this, they cast the ashes on the body of Ndun, and when the grave was filled the Creator said: "Go, and bring stones."

They fetched stones, and they put them on the grave, and the stones rose high, very high. The Creator said: "This is the Sign. When on your wanderings you see the spot where a man has been laid to rest, you shall cast on it a stone or a branch or a leaf. This shall you do."

...And when the stones were piled up high,

very high, very, very high, the Creator said to the people: "This is the parting, and you must part." So the people parted, some to the right, the others to the left; some went forward, others turned backward, and none remained.

And this was the first thing that happened.

The second thing was this. It happened at that moment when the people were about to separate. . . .

The Creator said to the people: "It is all over. I shall have nothing more to do with you."

They answered: "Pardon, oh, pardon! Thou art our father and our protector!" But the Creator answered them: "The spirit of the race will abide with you, strong and mighty."

. . . All the people went to their huts, and they slept. The next day, early in the morning, they returned to the council house and the Creator asked them: "Did you dream?". . .

And each man had seen the same animal that he had sacrificed to Ndun. . . .

The Creator said: "Take your sacrificial knives and draw your own blood."

Each took his sacrificial knife and drew his own blood. And he said again: "Take your sacrificial knives, and draw the blood of the animal . . . and mix it with your own."

And they did so.

But many were not content. All wanted to have the [leopard] for their blood-brother. So the Creator said: "Do not consider the outer body; each thing has its own virtue. I am your father."

And so it was done.

And on the morrow all parted, each with his own beast. The other animals went out into the forest, leaving the village where they had lived all together, and each established his own family. Each man left, taking his family with him, and there was no one left in the village, and each family had its own beast; it is into this that the virtue of the race enters after death. And that is why we Nduns all have the crocodile.

It is ended [Cendrars, 1921, pp. 32–34].

Examination of this myth reveals several themes:

1. Generational, or diachronic, conflict leads inexorably to conflict at the synchronic level and, as a result, to disintegration of the community as a whole, whereas simple synchronic conflict can be checked if the life of the community is organized along coherent traditional axes, which give strength and structure to succeeding generations.

2. Violence due to diachronic undifferentiation is violence without end (young against old and vice versa, *ad infinitum*). But there is tragic violence (which is, in fact, the archetype of all true tragedy), in which a serious situation of undifferentiation develops and radically disrupts established cultural ties. Consequently, there exists a profound loss of the guidelines governing self-identity. In this connection, the story clearly shows the diachronic confusion and lack of distinction with respect to sexual division. When neither order nor hierarchy prevails among living beings, the situation can indeed be characterized as precultural chaos.

3. To bring an end to the violence and establish a new cultural order, the mutual aggression within the group must be transferred onto a substitute, that is, polarized on a sacrificial victim.

4. The Ancestor's role is to serve as bearer of the Law and the Word, as supreme lawgiver of the new order, thus acting as intermediary between God and man.

In effect, the first part of the narrative tells of a socio-cultural order that has come full circle and is in jeopardy because it has become chaotic. It can be characterized, in particular, by the following features:

• the concentration of all human beings in a single place;

• peaceful coexistence with the animals;

• the closeness of God;

• conflict growing out of opposition between concrete diachronic series;

• but also, at the same time, the situation contains, *in posse*, elements prefiguring certain social and cultural forms of today.

It can be said that the development of the crisis or conflict retraces all the tragic ups and downs of "confusion," which, unchecked, leads to its ultimate consequence: the breakup of the whole community in the collapse of an old order that has clearly become unlivable for one and all. Even arbitration proves impossible, because there is no longer any stable frame of reference. The society has truly reached a crisis, with no turning back; there is nothing to do but create a new culture. Regarding the course of the cultural breakdown, which is localized at first within a well-defined sector of the group, one finds that the conflict spreads by degrees, reaching all the separate groups, and soon permeates entirely the most resistant structures of the community, to the extent of paralyzing all activity and, eventually, social life itself. From then on, the whole of reality is seized with an inchoate disorder, and no area of life can be protected from it any longer. The only thing to be done, then, is to build a new society out of the ashes of the old culture — a society that will be "peaceful" because it is "ordered" in accordance with new axes and new hierarchies, which put their stamp on the beginning of a consensus around a new group memory. In order to accomplish this — in terms of inculcating deep feelings for the new culture in one and all — the incipient society uses, as we have seen, the well-known mechanism of victimization, which will help to create the real substance of ancestral tradition.

In the second part of this Fang account, divinity proper is introduced. After performance of a series of archetypal acts, a new reality will come into being, which will acquire concreteness precisely from the ashes of the Ancestor (the "supreme victim" ordained by God), and those ashes will later become the ultimate referent for all that is sacred. As for the archetypal acts commanded or performed by God, they will form the paradigms of all significant human activities.

Clearly, a thorough analysis of this account alone would require a book to cover all the points I have put forward. Here, however, I should simply like to note that the action of the Creator is exerted in two areas.

1. In the category of soteriological knowledge:

•He classifies, differentiates, and identifies the essential things on the basis of which the world is structured and organized — there shall be a rational universe.

•He initiates men to a knowledge of plant and animal species, and to an understanding of various natural phenomena.

•He reveals to them that in unusually dire cultural situations, spirituality is the "royal road" to communication with the sacred (with divinity, actually, i.e., God and the Ancestor).

2. In the category of relations with the sacred:

•Specifically, ritual, of course, is always the fervent, "ecmnesic" commemoration of certain archetypal acts (culminating in sacrifice) that were performed when the current cultural and religious order was first established. These deeds are the doing of God himself, either directly or through the intermediary of a privileged being, appointed by God as founding Ancestor, only to be taken away later on — a pacificatory sacrifice — from the world of the living. Thus, after having gathered unto himself the one who will be the Ancestor, God unites, in a single outpouring of blood, representatives of the different antagonistic groups within the community that are at the root of the conflict. He thereby indicates that continual subversion of the specified ordering of signifiers in relation to the common Significate, that is, transgression of the Word (deep-seated rupture of the cultural bond ensuring mutual recognition of the identity of everyone within the specified difference), leads to a state of insecurity, to upheaval and disorder, in short, to a state of profound violence that can be transcended only with a new blood sacrifice. That is exactly the mechanism of sacrificial victimization.

•God introduces a certain continuity, at the symbolic

level, between man and animal, by showing men the substitute value of animals in terms of sacrifice.

•The words uttered by the Creator and repeated by those assembled set the pattern, in terms of their succession, for the oral liturgy that must always be a prominent feature at the offerings and blood sacrifices necessary for assuaging the state of diffuse violence accompanying cultural breakdown.

•Lastly, God confers on the Ancestor the rank of supreme lawgiver, at the level both of the lineage (family) and of the order (society). Thus the Ancestor stands alone in being above the "synchronic melee," while at the same time supporting the whole diachronic system. Thenceforth, the Ancestor will become the object of regular worship. One can see, then, how human biology bears the stamp of culture from the very beginning. It follows that, for Africans, the "biological," with respect to humankind, is absolutely inseparable from the cultural.

But we can also discern in this traditional tale another thematic constant in African mythology; after having performed the prototypic acts that laid the foundations of the present universe, God decided to withdraw from the affairs of this world. Thenceforth men would address themselves directly to the Ancestor, the tangible bearer of the divine Word and founder of the community through his sacrifice, which is remembered and commemorated. Here again we find the idea of God's remoteness, a theme I have already called attention to in a number of traditional African creation stories. I should like to note in passing that the special abode of the deceased, including those who are sacred, is the center of the earth and not the heavens, even though the sacred is evident in numerous symbols referring to things "on high," for all that rises always rises from a "center," which thus becomes the "center of the earth." One can therefore better understand the meaning of certain writers when they speak of the geocentrism of Africans, which is also, and at the same time, a form of anthropocentrism.

Before concluding this chapter, I should like to comment briefly on the episode concerning the construction of sacred space, as related in this mythical tale and as found in a number of traditional African scenarios.

In presenting a summary outline here, I should point out that according to the traditional spiritual conception, space cannot be thought of as a secular, "technical," uniform reality. On the contrary, it is made up of elements that are qualitatively different from one another, depending on their greater or lesser symbolic content. Occupation of a new area is always preceded by prior orientation in relation to a "center"; this center breaks the undifferentiated homogeneity of space, because to the traditional way of thinking, such undifferentiated homogeneity is comparable to natural (precultural) chaos.

This center itself, however, is inspired by the model of the archetypal construction of sacred space in primeval times. Mythic accounts tell of a place that served as the stage for some primordial event, crucial for the present human universe, and that belongs to a complex that also encompasses plant and animal species, minerals, and the founding Ancestor's remains

incorporated in the soil.[12] As the depository of essential
realities and truths, reaching down into the depths of
the earth and up to the sky, this ensemble is seen as the
"cosmic axis," which is also the "center of the world,"
place of conjunction and convergence, nodal point of
the entire universe. It is the only place where any real
rupture might occur in the links between vital elements
of a rational universe.

Therefore every altar, every place of worship, will be
constructed and consecrated in accordance with this archetypal model, with a view to recreating a replica of
this first sacred space of the beginning.

Similarly, the high symbolic content, so common in
Africa, of certain crossroads, localities, trees, rocks, and
other consecrated or hierophantic spaces — scaled-down
versions of the first space — is bound up with a much
vaster, far richer, and extremely complex religious-
symbolic whole.

The brief survey I have just attempted with respect to
certain symbols from the corpus of African mythology
barely affords a glimpse of the richness and complexity
of its content. Nevertheless, I should like to renew and
recapitulate certain ideas that are consonant with my
initial thinking.

1. Certain accounts inform us about some of the
characteristic elements that go to make up the concept
of person, with the ideal seeming to be essentially social
in nature. Man expresses his will to exist through the
affirmation of two main principles: *respect for cultural*

---

[12] Only ancestral substance, souls that have become spirits, and seeds can
penetrate the depths of the underworld.

order and — what amounts to the same thing — *respect for life*. His anthropological scheme seems to be oriented toward a search for plenitude, seen as an articulated whole, endowed with an open conscious in a social situation: a veritable interchange in which the different systems of close relations converge (from the horizontal network and the vertical network) and in which those systems are both integrated and extended. Such a view excludes any notion of strictly individualistic discontinuity, striving instead toward achieving the fullness of the human being in continuum, in close relationship with the poles consisting of:

•the Ancestors (verticality);
•the near and immediate family; and
•the community of reference (horizontality).

A personality so constructed, as well as its various layers, can be examined "psychologically" only in terms of its deeper involvement with its traditional cultural poles.

In humanizing nature from the beginning, African culture attempts to bring it within a more comprehensive order, embracing the whole of the universe.

This anthropological perspective expresses, in my opinion, absolute refusal to concede to chance — to contingency — the slightest real determination of human destiny. God having withdrawn, man's only destiny is precisely that which he makes for himself here on earth.

2. And yet, this universe that is rational and coherent, since it is "ensured" by God and founded on the Ancestor — a universe that gives identity and distinction (and hence security) to each traditional man and woman, precisely because it is not "flat" and homo-

geneous all over — was not so in the beginning. Instead, myths remind us that the present order of things (age sets, groups, institutions, etc.) and, more generally, the attainments of contemporary culture are built on a foundation of sacrificial violence, which itself grew out of the anarchy that once prevailed among concrete human ranks or sets. That confused situation could not be repeated in the future without mortal danger to one and all. Thus mythic accounts serve as reminders of the various vicissitudes of that formative violence: a state of diffuse violence that set in because a lack of distinction of the basic elements of identification of self and of others began to pervade the inchoate mass of the community in crisis. Myths refer to a precultural situation, with its succession of confrontations between ranks or sets and, within sets, between individuals, with murder, parricide, incest, etc., followed by the polarization of free aggressive tensions on scapegoats that become sacrificial victims.

The ritual complexes that are an extension of this category of myths are actually aimed at averting the original state of violence, which amounts to commemorating it in a ritualized group framework. It would seem, then, that one of the vital functions of sacred ritual is to ensure the maintenance of the cultural bond within the community by commemorating the violence of its origin. That violence is transferred onto a ritual victim through ritual sacrifice carried out collectively, which is the culmination of the ceremony celebrating the memory of the beginning.

This diffuse and constant threat, however, which so jeopardizes the cultural order of mankind and the security of one and all, is ever-present; at base, it can arise from each and any one of us. The Persecutor, man's enemy, has been man himself since the dawn of time. And myths suggest that he is none other than man's double, his complement, present in each of his constituent dimensions in various guises.[13]

This monstrous doubling is the danger in contemporary repetition of precultural archaisms; the double is the precultural being that has not yet become man, his "natural" twin, as it were, spirit of the bush, the forest, the lake, as opposed to man who has become man: man who defines himself as such by producing culture (cultural ties). He is above all a creature who, thanks to his accession to the symbolic and to the possession of symbols, classifies, distinguishes, separates, differentiates, contrasts, etc. The first creature — the natural being that antedates the human order in the strict sense — ceaselessly persecutes the second, that is, man as equated with culture.

In the beginning, according to a Hausa myth, God created numerous pairs of twins. At first everything went well on earth, but before long serious misunderstandings developed between the twins. As a result of these disputes, which threatened to destroy the whole community, God decided to separate the twins by making some of them invisible — these are the spirits — while their counterparts, men — the ancestors of present-day man — remained visible

[13]In terms of psychological and psychosocial representation (as opposed to mythology), we have already seen that the Enemy or Persecutor is indeed what could be called the invisible double of man himself in one or another of his constituent dimensions (verticality, horizontality, his own existence).

(a similar Hausa myth collected in Niger is reported by Monfouga-Nicolas, 1972, p. 46).

From this theme we can clearly see that the enemy is the double, the monstrous duplication of the self, invisible and still belonging to nature. In a way, this theme is the same as that of enemy brothers. And the creation of contemporary man (culture) is plainly the result of a crisis.

In the light of traditional tales, then, we come to understand that the fundamental problem for man is to succeed in mastering his other "self." If there is conflict between the human self (within) and the (natural) outside, which is an outside that has become natural and invisible, mental disturbance may then be manifested, which is therefore associated with a reappearance of the mythical violence that opens the way to disorder (death, disease, or misfortune) and which in itself, as we have seen, means a return to nature, to the unorganized, in short to the nonhuman.

Any affliction, which consequently can be none other than man's aggression in one of his constituent axes, evokes the earlier state of confusion and diffuse violence that marked the beginning. Strictly speaking, then, from the point of view of traditional societies, madness is not an illness but actually a mental problem that bears the name of aggression. The traditional conception of the personality is molar and synthetic, in radical contrast to a molecular, individualistic, and analytical view of the personality and its disturbances (defined, in the strict sense, as "autonomous" disorders). The idea of disease or disorder as autonomous is comprehensible only within the anthropological framework of an analytical, individualistic way of thinking, which separates things.

Making mental illness an autonomous, natural disorder of the individual subject, which can be analyzed separately, provides a facile excuse for excluding it theoretically and practically from the relational configurations and structures of actual present-day society. Quite easily, then, in intellectual good conscience, one "scientifically" disposes of the dynamics of the underlying systems that make up the personality as well as the real conflicts, only to concentrate, at best, on the analysis of imaginary conflicts or, at worst, on those involved in a supposedly purely biological development of disorders concerning self-identification and self-identity.

With the concept of victim that characterizes the African perspective, it is the whole community that is attacked (reenacting and reviving the primeval crisis), jeopardizing the order and structure of the institutional complex of relations (i.e., culture). That is why any therapeutic procedure must first be solidly based on a community (or at least a family) consensus before going on to symbolic practices aimed at triumphing over the aggression being inflicted, which throws everyone into question. To accomplish this requires the always perilous symbolic-technical manipulation of anti-human (natural) forces that are responsible for the human drama of mental illness, that is, the distortion of self-identification and self-identity.

In a more general way, it can be said that the attempt to achieve a comprehensive view of concrete human experience, because of the almost ineffable contradiction of that experience, leads precisely to a twofold problem, whose themes are simultaneously contradictory. In effect, it prompts one to "think"; that means not only does it call upon reason — comforting defensive rationalization? — but it also fosters unreason — pathetic delusion? Yet one thinks in terms of primary symbolic categories that are local and accessible, and which are the necessary basis of all communication and all language in actual social life. At another level, that concrete mass experience becomes expressible in a mode of complex symbolism, whereby it is recounted and reinterpreted in a tale, in myth, to be precise, which harbors such rich symbolic concretions.

Mythology, therefore, handed down to us from the beginning of time, is an account that is both orderly and irrational, a composite that elucidates, by analogy, the vicissitudes and dramas of people living today in terms of the primordial experience of the first founders. In the end, a bond is established and maintained between the living and the Ancestor. And it is that bond that defines culture and ensures it a solid foundation.

In my view, parallel to the objective and strictly historical study of human societies, the bringing to light and thorough analysis of certain themes and symbols contained in their myths and traditional tales will provide us access to the innermost structure of their cultural complex and hence to concrete human conduct as well as to the deep and latent psychic content that underlies this or that behavior.

In effect, the interest of certain mythic themes (major symbolic concretions) — if they are analyzed *in situ* in close connection with other elements of the culture of a society — lies in the fact that they lead us to the level of the structure of a total concrete experience and thereby mark out a major human field of precise meanings wherein dwells a concrete universal. On the contrary, dogmatic discourse, in so far as it is purportedly "always there" — short of, beneath, and beyond any real experience assignable to a concrete sociocultural universe — precedes, breaks down, and sums up all potential experience, in the name of some abstract universal of pure categories, which it assumes on its own, *a priori* and without a qualm, from its own origins.

Conclusion

From the structural point of view, according to our present knowledge, the universe that shapes the growth and development of the child, then molds the adolescent, and finally fashions the adult in Black Africa can be subdivided into three principal levels.

The level of concrete groups is divided along sexual lines into male and female groups. Within each of these groups (masculine/feminine) are ordered the successive age sets (the pyramid of ages). The groups and the sets each correspond to a position and to institutional functions that are culturally defined. Other differentiations, notably the division of community labor, also exist; they are superimposed on the first and primary framework of age classes or sets. Thus the whole edifice is organized in such a way that in the end great subtlety and precision are achieved, for one and all, in marking out personal identification within the groups of reference, within the more general ordering of all the concrete sets, and within other social differentiations. The peak of this complex ensemble is crowned with the Signified.

It follows that the relational networks that are interwoven within a given group between the various sections, sets, etc., are manifold, rich, and dense. But they always develop according to some order, in a certain direction, in conformity with a hierarchy and specific functions — a complete structure, a detailed and exhaustive description of which would far exceed the scope of the present study. In close correlation, at the level of mental activity: classifying, distinguishing, thoroughly knowing the place, the status, and the roles of everyone in the general language of the culture — all these operational categories emerge and are deployed as essential forms of learning in the development of the African child, whose intellect will be centered more on persons and the different types of relations concerning them than on inert external objects in the narrow sense. In my opinion, any construction of mental tests for African children should take this fundamental fact into account.

In Africa as elsewhere, it is possible to describe the concrete ways in which affective relations are institutionalized. Very quickly one perceives that there is an extremely fine and precise regulation of the personal affective flow between individuals in a systematized language, and models of such interchanges can be reconstructed, since they are readily identifiable with particularly intensive forms of communication. Thus there exist precise rules but also techniques that make it possible to resolve real or potential conflicts. What is most striking, in terms of day-to-day experience, is that atmosphere of security and highly personalized relations so commonly observed in the realm of practice.

At the level of dynamics proper, we have found that traditional education, whose psychological aspects have only begun to be systematically studied, develops along two major axes.

First of all, the process of identification is basically carried out in the age class or set (the locus of intense socialization and sociability), in terms of peers referring to their elders in the next set, and so on, the ultimate referent being, as we know, the Ancestor, true depository of the Word, of the Law, and hence of authority, and not at all the progenitive father as sire.

Then it becomes a matter, in terms of content, of living out real human relations, interspersed with the learning of symbols, statuses, and the like, and the division of labor. In this way the trajectory of the personality, which derives its initial impetus from the concept of person (represented by the person of the Ancestor, though matchless and unmatched), is in effect guided by the rule of succession of sets, which adds momentum to the normal dynamics of the alternation of successive generations. This coherent ensemble provides a foundation and a framework that ensure personal psychological maturity, which is, for that very reason, true sociocultural maturation, with no possible equivocation.

Lastly, within this institutional complex itself, an understanding of the mechanisms of personal psychological dynamics cannot be achieved without comparing them to the mechanisms of intracommunity dynamics. At a deeper level, that comes down to analyzing the states of aggressiveness and intragroup tensions or, more precisely, the conditions that threaten intragroup dynamics as such. This linkage between the individual and the collectivity seemed to me to be particularly consistent and obvious in this case. At the structural level, two basic patterns of traditional institutional operation can be described. I shall allude here especially to the last mythic theme I presented in Chapter 4.

1. Normally, in times of social (and personal) peace, the regular alternation of the generations in successive sets makes it possible to canalize practical everyday tensions on the synchronic level, i.e., within the same set, according to well-defined rules (ludic and/or ritual). That is a form of firm institutional control that everyone shares in and everyone respects. It works on the principle of the cathartic-dynamic pair: solidarity/competition (whether its expression be real, in play, or ritual) within a given set. Concomitantly, there are rules that conventionalize relations between successive sets.

2. Abnormally, conflictual tension overflows and becomes real opposition that is felt and expressed between successive sets. The resulting open diachronic tension blocks all institutional controls. The whole culture is threatened with destruction, and society goes mad, literally. This deep and genuine cultural rupture — owing to the anarchy concerning established positions, roles, etc. — reproduces, as we have seen, precultural chaos in the pathetic mode related in myths. On the practical everyday level, most people experience

a drifting, then a suspension of the foundations and markers of personal identification. It is in this sense that we can say that a "madman" is someone who is truly cut off from all living culture, with no projection into any possible future. He will have to have a new culture, that is, a whole new relational complex, which is accepted, and which is made up of new signifiers created according to a new order and based on a new signified. Therefore, at a certain level of analysis, the problem of madness is inextricable from the problem of culture as a whole.

And at the end of all these analyses, what have we learned? Essentially this: that understanding man, and especially man afflicted with mental illness, requires deepening our knowledge of the chain that forms him. Microscopic investigation of the mechanism of the illness already there should never make us forget that, more fundamentally, we must elucidate the problem of alienation itself. For more than a mechanism, madness is a problem, perhaps the problem — along with that of death — that is most basic to man. That is why the psychiatrist should always have the courage to tear himself away from the microscopic view of the isolated case — comforting, but how fragmentary — and face the problem of madness in its totality, because, after all, what it involves, ever and always, is the total man — with all the qualities that go to make him up for himself and for us — when he reorders his whole being in madness.

References

Abrahamsson, H. (1951), *The Origin of Death, Studies in African Mythology* (Studia Ethnographica Upsaliensia, 3). New York: Arno Press, 1977.

Adler, A. & Zempleni, A. (1972), *Le bâton de l'aveugle. Divination, maladie et pouvoir chez les Moundang du Tchad.* Paris: Hermann.

Afrique et Parole (1972), Les noms théophores. Déc. 1972, no. 38–40, 1.

Amon d'Aby, F. J. (1960), *Croyances religieuses et coutumes juridiques des Agni de la Côte d'Ivoire.* Paris: Larose.

Asuni, T. (1961), Suicide in Western Nigeria. In: *First Pan-African Psychiatric Conference* (Abeokuta, Nigeria, 12–18 nov., 1961), *Conference Report,* ed. T. A. Lambo. Ibadan, Nigeria: Government Printer, pp. 164–175.

—— (1968), Vagrant psychotics in Abeokuta. In: *Deuxième Colloque Africain de Psychiatrie* (Dakar, Senegal, 5–9 mars, 1968), *Compte rendu.* Paris: Audecam, pp. 115–123.

Atiwiya, G. (1971), Le "Zebola" (thérapie traditionelle des maladies mentales dans un cadre urbain). *Psychopathologie Africaine,* 7(3):389–416.

Ayats, H. (1968), Essai de différenciation statistique, selon des critères socio-culturels, d'une population de schizophrènes hospitalisés, délirants et non délirants. In: *Deuxième Colloque Africain de Psychiatrie* (Dakar, Senegal, 5–9 mars, 1968), *Compte rendu.* Paris: Audecam.

241

Ba, A. H. (1965), *Textes sacrés d'Afrique noire* (Collection UNESCO d'oeuvres representatives; Série africaine), ed. G. Dieterlen. Paris: Gallimard, pp. 7–13 (Preface).

_____ & Dieterlen, G. (1961), *Koumen, texte initiatique des pasteurs peul* (Cahiers de l'Homme). Paris: Mouton.

Baasher, T. A. (1961), Some Aspects of the History of the Treatment of Mental Disorders in the Sudan. Paper distributed at the First Pan-African Psychiatric Conference, Abeokuta, Nigeria, 12–18 Nov., 1961.

Baker, A. P. (1959), La santé mentale au Nyassaland. In: *Santé mentale* (Rapport B.P.I.T.T., publ. no. 3/T, juillet 1959). Léopoldville: Bureau Permanent Inter-Africain de la Tsé-Tsé et de la Trypanosomiase.

Balandier, G. (1955), *The Sociology of Black Africa: Social Dynamics in Central Africa*, trans. D. Garman. New York: Praeger, 1970.

Bastide, R. (1956), La causalité externe et la causalité interne dans l'explication sociologique. *Cahiers Internationaux de Sociologie*, 21:77–99.

_____ (1960a), *The African Religions of Brazil: Toward a Sociology of the Interpenetration of Civilizations*, trans. H. Sebba. Baltimore: Johns Hopkins University Press, 1978.

_____ (1960b), Problèmes de l'entrecroisement des civilisations et de leurs oeuvres. In: *Traité de sociologie* (vol.2), ed. G. Gurvitch. Paris: Presses Universitaires de France, pp. 315–330.

Beattie, J. (1964), Divination in Bunyoro, Uganda. *Sociologus*, 14:44–62.

Bernard, A. M. (1962), Le mystère du nom. *Lectio Divina*, no. 35.

Bourguignon, E. (1968), Divination, transe et possession en Afrique transsaharienne. In: *La divination* (vol. 2), ed. A. Caquot & M. Leibovici. Paris: Presses Universitaires de France, pp. 331–358.

Buakasa, G. (1971), *La Kindoki et les Nkisi*. Thèse de 3e Cycle, Université de Paris (EPHE).

_____ (1972), Histoire d'un lignage. Lecture symptômale des origines et de l'histoire d'un lignage. *Cahiers des Religions Africaines*, 6(12):156–179.

Caquot, A. & Leibovici, M., eds. (1968), *La divination*. Paris: Presses Universitaires de France.

Carothers, J. C. (1947), A study of mental derangement in Africans, and an attempt to explain its peculiarities, more especially in relation to the African attitude to life. *J. Ment. Sci.*, 93:548–597.

_____ (1951), Frontal lobe function and the African. *J. Ment. Sci.* 97:12–48.

_____ (1953), *The African Mind in Health and Disease: A Study in Ethnopsychiatry* (World Health Organization Monograph Series, no. 17). New York: Negro Universities Press, 1970.

Cazeneuve, J. (1971), *Sociologie du rite*. Paris: Presses Universitaires de France.

Cendrars, B. (1921), *The African Saga*, trans. M. Bianco. New York:

Negro Universities Press, 1969 (reprint of 1927 ed.).

Colin, R. (1965), *Littérature africaine d'hier et de demain*. A.D.E.C.

Collomb, H. (1965a), Assistance psychiatrique en Afrique (expérience sénégalaise). *Psychopathologie Africaine*, 1(1):11–84.

———— (1965b), Bouffées délirantes en psychiatrie africaine. *Psychopathologie Africaine*, 1(2):167–239.

———— (1966), Aspects particuliers de la psychiatrie africaine. In: *Cliniques africaines*, ed. M. Payet, P. Pène, M. Sankalé et al. Paris: Gauthier-Villars, pp. 419–431.

———— & Zwingelstein, J. (1962), Les états dépressifs en milieu africain (Dakar). *Information Psychiatrique*, (6, juin 1962):515–527.

Dadié, B. (1970), *Béatrice du Congo*. Paris: Présence Africaine.

Dieterlen, G. (1951), *Essai sur la religion bambara*. Paris: Presses Universitaires de France.

Dika Akwa (1971), *La sphère du sacré en Afrique*. Thèse de 3e Cycle, Université de Paris (VII).

Diop, B. (1947), *Tales of Amadou Koumba*, trans. D. S. Blair. London: Oxford University Press, 1966.

———— (1960), *Leurres et lueurs* (2e éd.). Paris: Présence Africaine, 1967.

Diop, M. (1961), La dépression chez le Noir africain. *Psychopathologie Africaine*, 1967, 3(2):183–194.

———— (1968), De la transplantation négro-africaine en France. *Psychopathologie Africaine*, 4(2):227–276.

———— Zempleni, A., Martino, P. & Collomb, H. (1964), Signification et valeur de la persécution dans les cultures africaines. In: *Congrès de Psychiatrie et de Neurologie de Langue Française* (Marseilles, 7–12 sept., 1964), *Comptes rendus*, ed. P. Warot. Paris: Masson, pp. 333–343.

Doutreloux, A. (1967), *L'ombre des fétiches, société et culture Yombe*. Louvain, Belgium: Nauwelaerts.

Eliade, M. (1957), *Mythes, rêves et mystères*. Paris: Gallimard.

Erny, P. (1972), *L'enfant et son milieu en Afrique noire*. Paris: Payot.

Evans-Pritchard, E. E. (1937), *Witchcraft, Oracles and Magic among the Azande*. Oxford: Clarendon Press.

Ey, H. (1958), Les problèmes cliniques des schizophrénies. *L'Evolution Psychiatrique*, fasc. 2 (avril-juin):149–211.

Gaisseau, P. D. (1953), *La forêt sacrée*. Paris: Albin-Michel.

Giel, R. (1968), Psychiatric morbidity in Ethiopia. In: *Deuxième Colloque Africain de Psychiatrie* (Dakar, Senegal, 5–9 mars, 1968), *Compte rendu*. Paris: Audecam.

———— & Van Luijk, J. N. (n.d.), *The Epidemiology of Mental Illness in Ethiopia* (Monograph Series I). Addis Ababa: Haile Selassie University of Addis Ababa.

Girard, R. (1972), *La violence et le sacré*. Paris: Grasset.

Gluckman, M. (1955), *Custom and Conflict in Africa*. New York: Barnes

& Noble, 1964.

Gravrand, H. (1966), Le "Lup" serer. Phénoménologie d l'emprise des Pangol et psychothérapie des "possédés." *Psychopathologie Africaine*, 2(2):195–226.

Griaule, M. (1948), *Conversations with Ogotemmêli: An Introduction to Dogon Religious Ideas*. London: Oxford University Press, 1965.

_____ & Dieterlen, G. (1965), *Le renard pâle* (Université de Paris. Travaux et mémoires de l'Institut d'Ethnologie, no. 72). Paris: Institut d'Ethnologie.

Haworth (1968), Schizophrenia, hysteria and other barriers to communication. In: *Deuxième Colloque Africain de Psychiatrie* (Dakar, Senegal, 5–9 mars, 1968), *Compte rendu*. Paris: Audecam, pp. 44–57.

Hébert, J. C. (1961), Analyse structurale des géomancies comoriennes, malgaches et africaines. *Journal de la Société des Africanistes*, 31(fasc. 2):115–208.

Heusch, L. de (1965), *Les religions africaines traditionelles*. Paris: Seuil.

_____ (1971), *Pourquoi l'épouser? et autres essais*. Paris: Gallimard.

Holas, B. (1948), Moyens de protection magique chez les Lébou. *Notes Africaines*, no. 39(juillet): 19–24.

_____ (1956), Fondements spirituels de la vie sociale sénoufo. *Journal de la Société des Africanistes*, 26(1–2):9–32.

_____ (1964), Mythologies des origines en Afrique noire. *Diogène*, 48(oct.–déc.):102–119.

Jahn, J. (1958), *Muntu: An Outline of the New African Culture*, trans. M. Grene. New York: Grove Press, 1961.

Janzen, J. M. (1969), Vers une phénoménologie de la guérison en Afrique centrale. *Etudes Congolaises* (ONRD, Kinshasha), 12(2, avril-juin): 97–114.

Jaouen, R. (n.d.), Le mythe de la retraite de Bumbouloun chez les Giziga du Nord Cameroun—la nomination de Dieu. *Afrique et Parole*, no. 33–34:56–57.

Jaulin, R. (1966), *La géomancie, analyse formelle* (Cahiers de l'Homme). Paris: Mouton.

Junod, H. A. (1912), *The Life of a South African Tribe* (2 vols.). New Hyde Park, N.Y.: University Books, 1962 (reprint of 2nd rev. ed., 1927).

Kagame, A. (1968–1969), La place de Dieu et de l'homme dans la religion des Bantu. *Cahiers des Religions Africaines*, 2(4, juillet 1968):213–222; 3(5, janvier 1969): 5–11.

Kane, C. H. (1961), *Ambiguous Adventure*, trans. K. Woods. New York: Walker, 1963.

Kenyatta, J. (1938), *Facing Mount Kenya: The Life of the Gikuyu*. New York: AMS Press, 1978 (reprint of 1953 edition).

Ki-Zerbo, J. (1972), *Histoire de l'Afrique noire*. Paris: Haitier.

Kouyate, S. B. (1964), *Les dirigeants d'Afrique noire face à leur peuple*.

Paris: F. Maspero.

Labouret, H. (1922), La divination en Afrique noire. *L'Anthropologie*, 31:334–360.

Lambo, T. A. (1961), A form of social psychiatry in Africa. *World Mental Health*, 13(4):190–203.

———— (1968), Schizophrenia: Its features and prognosis in the African. In: *Deuxième Colloque Africain de Psychiatrie* (Dakar, Senegal, 5–9 mars, 1968), *Compte rendu*. Paris: Audecam.

Lamont, A. M. & Blignault, W. J. (1953), A study of male Bantu admissions at Weskoppies during 1952. *S. Afr. Med. J.*, 27:637–639.

Lapassade, G. (1963), *L'entrée dans la vie*. Paris: Editions de Minuit.

Laye, C. (1953), *The Dark Child*, trans. J. Kirkup & E. Jones. New York: Farrar, Straus & Giroux, 1969.

Lebeuf, J. P. (1958), Santé mentale et "possession." In: *Désordres mentaux et santé mentale en Afrique au sud du Sahara/Mental Disorders and Mental Health in Africa South of the Sahara* (CCTA/CSA-WFMH-WHO Meeting of Specialists on Mental Health, Bukavu) (Scientific Council for Africa South of the Sahara, publ. no. 35). London: Commission for Technical Co-operation in Africa South of the Sahara, pp. 164–167.

———— (1961), *L'habitation des Fali*. Paris: Hachette.

Lehmann, J. P. & Memel Foté, H. (1967), Le cercle du prophète et du sorcier. *Psychopathologie Africaine*, 3(1):81–119.

Leroux, H. (1948), Animisme et Islam dans la subdivision de Maradi. *Bulletin de l'Institut Français d'Afrique Noire*, 10:595–695.

Lévi-Strauss, C. (1958), *Structural Anthropology*, trans. C. Jacobson & B. G. Schoepf. New York: Basic Books, 1963.

Liénart, G. (1968), La signification du nom chez les peuples bantu. *La Langage et l'Homme*, no. 7 (mai):43–54.

Lombard, J. (1967), Les cultes de possession en Afrique noire et le Bori Hausa. *Psychopathologie Africaine*, 3(3):419–439.

Malonga, J. (1954), La légende de M'foumou Ma Mazano. Extracted in: *Anthologie négro-africaine* (Collection Marabout Université, no. 129), ed. L. Kesteloot. Verviers, Belgium: Gérard, 1967, pp. 200–203.

Maquet, J. (1962), *Civilizations of Black Africa*, rev. and trans. J. Rayfield. New York: Oxford University Press, 1972.

Matip, B. (1962), L'homme-grenouille. In: *Anthologie négro-africaine* (Collection Marabout Université, no. 129), ed. L. Kesteloot. Verviers, Belgium: Gérard, 1967, pp. 363–366.

Maupoil, B. (1961), *La géomancie à l'ancienne Côte des Esclaves* (Travaux et Mémoires de l'Institut d'Ethnographie, no. 42). Paris: Institut d'Ethnographie.

Memel Foté, H. (1962), Rapport sur la civilisation animiste. In: *Colloque sur les religions*. Paris: Présence Africaine, pp. 31–58.

Mercier, P. (1966), *Histoire de l'anthropologie*. Paris: Presses Universitaires de France, 1971.

Moffson, A. (1955), A study of 400 consecutive male Bantu admissions to Weskoppies Hospital. *S. Afr. Med. J.*, 29:689–692.

Monfouga-Nicolas, J. (1972), *Ambivalence et culte de possession*. Paris: Anthropos.

Monteil, C. (1931), La divination chez les Noires de l'Afrique occidentale française. *Bulletin du Comité d'Etudes Historiques et Scientifiques de l'Afrique Occidentale Française*, 14(1–2): 72–136.

Murdock, G. P. (1959), *Africa: Its Peoples and Their Cultural History*. New York: McGraw-Hill.

Ngoma, F. (1963), *L'initiation Ba-Kongo et sa signification*. Paris: Centre d'étude des problèmes sociaux indigènes, Collection de mémoires.

Niane, D. T. (1960), *Sundiata: An Epic of Old Mali*, trans. G. D. Pickett. London: Longman Group, 1965.

Ortigues, M. -C. & Ortigues, E. (1966), *Oedipe africain* (rev. ed.). Paris: Union Générale d'Editions, 1973.

Paques, V. (1954), *Les Bambara*. Paris: Presses Universitaires de France.

Park, G. K. (1963), Divination and its social contexts. *J. Royal Anthropological Inst.*, 93(2):195–209.

Parrinder, G. (1967), *African Mythology*. London: Paul Hamlyn.

Paulme, D. (1954), *Les gens du riz: les Kissi de Haute-Guinée* (2e éd.). Paris: Plon, 1970.

——— (1956), Oracles grecs et devins africains. *Revue d'Histoire des Religions*, 159:145–157.

——— ed. (1971), *Classes et associations d'âge en Afrique de l'Ouest*. Paris: Plon.

Pidoux, C. (1954), Les rites de possession en pays Zerma (Niger). *Comptes Rendus des Séances de l'Institut Français d'Anthropologie* (séance du 17 nov., 1954, Paris), fasc. 8, no. 99.

Poynter, F. N. L. (1971), Médecine africaine. In: *Médecines traditionelles et art d'Afrique noire*, ed. J. Sonolet. Paris: Expansion Scientifique Française, pp. 5–9 (Introduction).

Prince, R. (1962), Frequency of depressions in African natives (comments on M. J. Field's book, *Search for Security*; Evanston, Ill.: Northwestern University Press, 1961). *Review and Newsletter; Transcultural Research in Mental Health Problems* (McGill University), 13(Oct. 1962):42–50.

Rattray, R. S. (1927), *Religion and Art in Ashanti*. Oxford: Clarendon Press.

Retel-Laurentin, A. (1969), *Oracles et ordalies chez les Nzakara*. Paris: Mouton.

Roche, J. -L. (1972), Possession et délivrance chez les Lebous du Cap-Vert et du Diander (Sénégal). *Bulletin de Psychologie*, 25(302, 18):1057–1062.

Rouch, J. (1960), *La religion et la magie Songhay*. Paris: Presses Universitaires de France.

Sadji, A. (1955), *Nini, mulâtresse du Sénégal*. Paris: Présence Africaine, 1965.

Sangmuah, E. (1968), The healing (spiritual) therapy in Ghana, Ankaful Hospital, Ghana. In: *Deuxième Colloque Africain de Psychiatrie* (Dakar, Senegal, 5–9 mars, 1968), *Compte rendu*. Paris: Audecam, pp. 104–111.

Senghor, L. S. (1959), Eléments constitutifs des civilisations négro-africaines. *Présence Africaine*, no. 24–25:244–282.

Shepherd, M., Cooper, B., Brown, A. C. & Kalton, G. (1967), Maladie mentale et médecine générale: Conclusions. *Revue de Médecine Psychosomatique et de Psychologie Médicale*, 9(4):259–276.

Silla, O. (1967), *Croyances et cultes syncrétiques des Lébous du Sénégal*. Thèse du 3e Cycle, Université de Paris.

Sonolet, J. (1971), *Médecines traditionelles et art d'Afrique noire* (Entretiens de Bichat, Faculté de Médecine, Pitié-Salpêtrière, Paris, 3–10 oct., 1971). Paris: Expansion Scientifique Française.

Sow, D. (1962), *Les conduites auto-agressives: suicide et auto-mutilation au Sénégal*. Thèse de Médecine. Université de Dakar.

Sow, I. (1977), *Psychiatrie dynamique africaine* (Bibliothèque scientifique). Paris: Payot.

Storper-Perez, D. (1968), *L'hospitalisation en milieu psychiatrique occidental, fait et facteur d'acculturation chez les Wolof du Sénégal*. Thèse de 3e Cycle, Université de Paris, Sorbonne.

Thomas, L. -V. & Luneau, P. (1975), *La terre africaine et ses religions*. Paris: Larousse.

Tiarko Fourche, J. A. & Morlighem, H. (1939), *Les communications des indigènes du Kasai avec les âmes des morts*. Brussels: Falk.

Tooth, G. (1950), *Studies in Mental Illness in the Gold Coast* (Colonial Research Publications, no. 6). London: M. H. Stationery Office.

Towo-Atangana, G. (1967), Nged-nso-fa. In: *Anthologie négro-africaine* (Collection Marabout Université, no. 129), ed. L. Kesteloot. Verviers, Belgium: Gérard, pp. 335–338.

Turner, V. W. (1968), *The Drums of Affliction: A Study of Religious Processes among the Ndembu of Zambia*. Oxford: Clarendon Press and the International African Institute.

Vernant, J. -P. (1974), Parole et signes muets. In: *Divination et rationalité*, ed. J.-P. Vernant et al. Paris: Editions du Seuil, pp. 9–25.

Wing, J. van (1921), *Etudes Bakongo: sociologie – religion et magie* (2nd ed.). Bruges: Desclée de Brouwer, 1938.

Woodbury, M. A. (1966), Comprehensive psychiatry in Nigeria: The village care system. *Hosp. Community Psychiat.*, Vol. 17.

Zahan, D. (1960), *Sociétés d'initiation bambara: le N'domo, le Korè*.

Paris: Mouton.

_____ (1970), *The Religion, Spirituality, and Thought of Traditional Africa*, trans. K. E. Martin & L. M. Martin. Chicago: University of Chicago Press, 1979.

Zempleni, A. (1968), *L'interprétation et la thérapie traditionelle du désordre mental chez les Wolof et les Lébou du Sénégal*. Thèse de 3e Cycle, Université de Paris.

_____ (1969), La thérapie traditionelle des troubles mentaux chez les Wolof et les Lébou (Sénégal): principes. *Social Science and Medicine*, 3:191–205.

Zempleni-Rabain, J. (1966), Modes fondamentaux de relations chez l'enfant wolof du sevrage a l'intégration dans la classe d'âge. *Psychopathologie Africaine*, 2(2):143–177.

_____ (1974), L'enfant wolof de 2 à 5 ans. *Thérapie Psychomotrice*, (23):27–44.